HOW TO
BUY & SELL REAL ESTATE
WITHOUT
USING A BANK!

Advanced
Seller Financing Techniques
And "Green Mortgages"

Book #2 of the
"Highest and Best
Real Estate Investment"
Series

MICHAEL P. WATSON
with
JENNIFER HAWKINS

MIKE WATSON
PUBLISHING

Limit of Liability/Disclaimer of Warranty. While the publisher and authors have used their best efforts in preparing this book, they make no representations or warranties with respect to the accuracy or completeness of the contents of this book. The advice and strategies contained herein may not be suitable for your situation. This book is intended as a reference volume only in the areas of real estate investing. The information given here is to help you make informed decisions when buying, selling and financing real estate; it is not intended as a substitute for or to replace the advice of a qualified professional, such as a lawyer, accountant, real estate broker, architect or licensed contractor. Some of the information contained in this book may be affected by changes in interpretations of the law or deviations in market conditions in specific geographic areas. The forms contained in this book are for illustration only and are not intended for actual use. The authors and publisher specifically disclaim any liability arising directly or indirectly from the use of this book. Neither the publisher nor authors shall be liable for any loss of profit or any other commercial damages, including but not limited to special, incidental, consequential, or other damages. There are inherent risks in any type of investment. Investors should proceed with caution and any results in the book are not guaranteed and are not typical.

HOW TO BUY AND SELL REAL ESTATE WITHOUT USING A BANK!
Copyright © 2009 MIKE WATSON PUBLISHING L.L.C. All rights reserved. Printed in the United States. No part of this publication may be reproduced, stored in a retrieval system, or transmitted, in any form or by any means, electronic, mechanical, photocopying, recording, or otherwise, without the prior written permission of the publisher.

Published by: Mike Watson Publishing L.L.C.

For more information regarding this book and the authors, please contact the Mike Watson Companies at (866) WATSON-5, or visit www.MikeWatsonCompanies.com.

FIRST EDITION

Designed by Nathan Stitt

Library of Congress Cataloging-in-Publication Data
Watson, Michael P.
How to Buy and Sell Real Estate Without Using a Bank:
Advanced Seller Financing Techniques and "Green Mortgages".
Michael P. Watson with Jennifer Hawkins

Library of Congress: 2008911895
ISBN-13: 978-0-9800827-4-6
ISBN-10:   0-9800827-4-9

<u>Acknowledgements</u>

This book is dedicated to my beautiful wife Heather Kristine Watson and my wonderful children Madison, Jaylin, Chloe, Hunter and Isabel. I also dedicate this book to my parents Brent and Pam Watson who taught me to dream big and fight hard. Thanks to my wonderful staff at Mike Watson Investing LLC who have helped immensely with this project. I also dedicate this book to the fantastic student investors who have given me more than I'll ever be able to give them. Lastly to Jennifer Hawkins, my co-author, who has tirelessly worked to bring our dream to fruition.

- Michael P. Watson

Thank you for your unwavering support and awesome edits Connie Randmaa (Mom), thanks for all you do in my life to keep me inspired Mark, Connor, and Brannon Hawkins. Thanks to Nate Stitt, my "Power Team" and all of the wonderful student investors at MWI you make this work possible and a pleasure. And finally, thank you Mike Watson, for your never-ending belief and faith in others.

- Jennifer Hawkins

CONTENTS

INTRODUCTION
Overview of "The Foundation to Success" 3

CHAPTER 1
**How is the "Highest and Best" use related
to seller financing?** 17

CHAPTER 2
Open your mind to the possibilities! 25

CHAPTER 3
What is seller financing? 35

CHAPTER 4
**Seller financing is better for the seller
than it is for the buyer** 43

CHAPTER 5
Isn't seller financing risky? 59

CHAPTER 6
9 Ways to Seller Finance Properties 67

CHAPTER 7
The 10th Way to Seller Finance Properties 83

CHAPTER 8
How does the paperwork work? 91

CHAPTER 9

You can create ANYTHING with seller financing 97

CHAPTER 10

"Green" mortgages... 105

CHAPTER 11

**The 23 Most Powerful Terms to Negotiate
with Seller Financing** 113

CHAPTER 12

**Can a seller really finance 100% of the price
if there is a loan on the property?**.................... 135

CHAPTER 13

Back-Up Plans or... Drop that "Due on Sale Clause"...... 143

CHAPTER 14

**The "Top 2" Places to Find Sellers who are
RIPE for Giving You Seller Financing!
(Bonus Topic: The Perfect Storm)**...................... 155

CHAPTER 15

**4 Other Places to Find Sellers who are
RIPE for Giving You Seller Financing** 175

CHAPTER 16

How to Get the Seller to "See the Light"....................... 189

CHAPTER 17

Power of the "4-Offer Spreadsheet" 199

CHAPTER 18
De-collateralization or....
Raising Capital the Fun Way 213

CHAPTER 19
Do Not Forget These 5 Vital Techniques! 219

CHAPTER 20
My "Secret" Goal 235

CHAPTER 21
The "One Hit Wonder" or...
Property-less Passive Income for Life 241

Appendix 1: Frequently asked Questions 255
Appendix 2: Investor Tools 265

OVERVIEW OF "THE FOUNDATION TO SUCCESS"

OVERVIEW OF "THE FOUNDATION TO SUCCESS"

This is the second book in my series of books based on "The Highest and Best Real Estate Investment". The first book is an overview of my entire program. It goes over my ten step system called "The Foundation to Success". It teaches novice and professional investors how to find, buy, improve, and *profit* from properties which are *not currently* utilizing their "Highest and Best" use.

> **"Highest and Best" Use** – A property which is utilizing its maximum density available based on the underlying zoning.
>
>   Definition

I highly recommend you read my first book titled "The Highest and Best Real Estate Investment – How to Make Million Dollar Profits in the 21st Century" prior to reading this book. It will teach you the fundamentals of my system as well as the specific details you can use today to start and complete successful real estate investments. I will cover several of the concepts from the first book in this book, but will not go over the entire system in detail.

In "The Highest and Best Real Estate Investment", I teach the ins and outs of the 10 steps of "The Foundation to Success". These steps along with a short explanation are as follows:

Step #1... Know "The Foundation to Success"

I suggest you memorize "The Foundation to Success". If you are
not enjoying the life you wish to live then you either don't have the
knowledge you need yet or you are unwilling to use it. If you don't
have it, keep reading. If you are unwilling to use your knowledge,
then my goal is to give you enough information, examples and guid-
ance for you to feel like you can take action now.

> **The Foundation to Success** - Ten steps for real estate investing
> success. This is the process by which profits are made in the short-term
> and equity, net worth and multiple streams of cash flow are created in
> the long-term.
>
> Definition

Step #2... Create your "Red Button Statement"

In order to be a powerful investor you must be clear about "Why"
you are investing and for "Whom" you are investing. To be successful
in real estate investing you must have a powerful reason to drive you
through times both thick and thin. Why are you reading this book?
Do you want to stay where you are or would you like to improve your
current situation? Your "Red Button Statement" will help you become
more passionate about your success. Your "Red Button Statement"
will also help you sustain that passion when things get tough.

Your personal statement can go something like this, "I will continue
to invest in real estate until I have _____for myself and _____
___" You can fill in the blanks with your own "why" and "who". For
instance, you could insert "created $5000 a month of passive income"
and "my wife and children". The more people you include in this statement the better. The more personally involved you are in this process,
the more powerful it will be. Create your "Red Button Statement" so

you have something to rely on when the going gets tough.

> **Red Button Statement** - A statement that an investor creates which elicits passion, enthusiasm and action in his/her investing career. The statement spells out the reasons for action and serves as an emotional mission statement.
>
> Definition

Step #3... Find Incredible Properties Using Competing and Non-competing Methods

This step includes detailed information on how to find properties. It also goes over exactly where to look and what to look for when you are out in the field.

Locating a property means knowing what a great deal is in today's market. Typically you will do well with lower-end income-producing property in a buyer's market. In 2009 we are in a buyer's market in many locations.

> **Buyer's Market** – A market where the prices are down or falling and there is an abundance of inventory. The buyer has more power in most negotiations because of the amount of product from which to select.
>
> Definition

In my first book I teach you the different kinds of income-producing properties which have a "Higher and Better" use and exactly how to find an abundance of them. Hint: you drive by them every day. Another tip is to find properties that are corporate owned and then buy the corporation. (Talk about seller financing! More on this later.)

Finally in this step I teach you how to create your "Area of Expertise". This explains the most important criteria for choosing the area where you will do your first 10-20 deals. Also it has the full "Area of Expertise" campaign you can use to start to bring in these great deals!

> **Area of Expertise** - A physical area on which an investor chooses to focus due to the availability of distressed properties, zoning incentives, "Highest and Best" uses and development standards. The investor will initiate a campaign to buy properties in this area for short-term and long-term profits.
>
> Definition

Step #4... Evaluate Properties for Their "Highest and Best" Use

In "The Foundation to Success" I teach you how to find properties that are not currently using their "Highest and Best" use. That is because when you change them to their "Highest and Best" use then you will *increase their value.*

You learn to evaluate the property both for what it is now *and* for what it can be turned into in the future. In other words you are going to evaluate it for its *"Highest and Best"* use. I then teach you how to evaluate a deal for the possible profits in the "short-term", or for its "long-term" potential. By using these evaluations you can determine approximately what will happen if you sell now or hold the property in your long term portfolio.

Step #5... Buy the Property Using the Two OPM's

Never use your *own* cash again! In this step I teach you ways to buy property using "Other People's Money" *and* "Other People's Mortgages" (OPM'S). These include incredible techniques for seller financing *any property*. In addition you learn how to create assumable (recyclable or "green") mortgages.

One of the best ways to create a "Higher and Better" property is to manipulate the *terms* of the deal. For example, you could buy a property with 100% seller financing and make it assumable. Then you could sell the property at a higher interest rate and profit by earning the spread between the two rates plus the down payment.

This step will help you raise all of the capital you need for any deal. In the book you're reading now on seller financing, I will turn you into an expert on this step of "The Foundation to Success". Think how many properties you could buy if you knew how to get financing from sellers instead of relying on a bank.

In addition, how many more properties could you sell and how quickly could you sell them if you knew how to *offer* your own financing to every buyer who was *interested*....not just *qualified*.

How many current mortgages that are going bad could be saved? This knowledge of seller financing will give you the tools and the power to change the market. It will enable you to do fantastic deals *and* help others.

Seller financing can create cash profits, equity positions and cash flow like no other tool that is available in real estate investing. In this book I will teach you how to be a master at seller financing!

Step #6... *Expose* the vision!

Immediately put your investment back up for sale at the "Higher and Better" price by exposing your "vision" of what the property will be. What this means is that you have purchased a property with a "Higher and Better" use, using other people's money, and are now going to show everyone else in the market why you bought the property. You will be putting it up for sale as the "Higher and Better" property that it can soon become. This is my "Flixer" technique in a nut shell.

> **Flixer** - A real estate investment where the fixer-upper process has begun but is sold for a profit before the work is complete. A Flixer exposes the "Higher and Better" use of a property to others and thus makes the property more valuable.
>
> Definition

Step #7... Create and Enhance Equity

This step is when you change the use of the property, and *explode* your profits and equity. I go into great detail about many of the ways you can change the use of different types of properties into their "Higher and Better" use. I talk about the different ways to "fix-up" properties so they are at their highest value.

> **Equity** - The monetary value found by subtracting a property's debts from the current value.
>
> Definition

Included are ways to change a property by just exposing a different concept such as using a property as condominiums rather than apartments. Another example is to simply do paperwork and change the value of a property. For instance, you could do a lot split or create a flag lot.

> **Flag Lot** – A lot that is subdivided into two separate lots. There is a front lot and a back lot with a driveway going down the side of the front lot. The Back lot is in the shape of a flag and the driveway is the pole.
>
> Definition

EXAMPLE OF A FLAG LOT

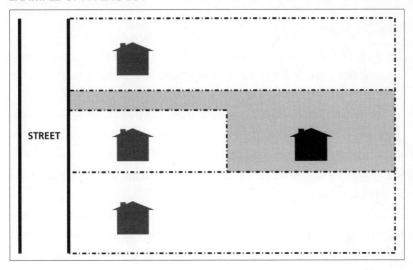

Next I teach you how to physically change a property to make it worth more such as a "floor plan fixer-upper". And finally I go over how to do many different types of "terms fixer uppers".

Step #8... Sell the Property for a Profit

This is your "short-term" plan for *fast cash*. I teach you specific techniques on how to find the "next user" and market to them directly while marketing to the "end user" at the same time. I taught a 3 day course in Hawaii on this topic alone and have not had a chance to repeat it! These techniques are all included in the first book and will dramatically increase your chances of selling your property.

Next User – The next person who will perform work on the property such as an appraiser, lender, contractor, roofer etc.

End User – The person who purchases the property to use it for its final intended "Highest and Best" use.

Definition

Step #9... Refinance for an Equity Position.

Here is where you become an expert on how to have all of the different types of income or assets that create true wealth. I go into your long-term strategy for passive income and how to have cash flow forever *without* owning property!

You learn how to take some cash from your deals and how to have gigantic equity positions to use to your benefit. You also learn awesome strategies for having positive cash flow from income producing property and finally, for creating long term income from notes receivable.

This is an extremely powerful technique that is not usually taught to investors. It is your "ace in the hole" for making sure that every deal will work. Since you always evaluate a property allowing for this outcome you are insuring that your deals have a back-up plan if they don't sell in the short-term.

Step #10... Prosper and Share with Others.

In this step I teach you how to achieve fantastic profits and cash flows with greater leverage using *"Power Teams"*. I teach you how to do a deal, get paid well and pay others too! This is my ultimate definition of wealth. By having a power team you will not only do more deals faster but the rewards you all reap will be a constant source of gratification.

I have many students who have power teams. Some even have family members on their teams. I teach you who the vital people are that you must have on your team as well as how to involve *anyone* interested in real estate investing.

> **Power Team** - A group of real estate investors who work together to achieve a common goal of investing success. The group pools their time, talents and financial abilities in their pursuit of success.
>
> Definition

As you can see, this book, "How to Buy and Sell Real Estate without Using a Bank" by itself, is not a comprehensive investing guide. It is simply an in-depth explanation and "how-to" guide for Step #5 of "The Foundation to Success". As mentioned previously, it is extremely important for a real estate investor to intimately know all of these ten steps. When you do and then take action they will launch you into success.

The "Highest and Best" Real Estate Investment!

For a comprehensive look at my entire investing system and the "Foundation to Success", check out my first book.
This book is called *The "Highest and Best" Real Estate Investment!*.
You can buy this book on Amazon.com, or on my website at
www.MikeWatsonInvesting.com.

The market is now ready for seller financing like it has not been since the late 1970's when interest rates were over 15% and nobody wanted to get a traditional loan. People are having trouble getting traditional lenders to give them loans. These buyers still want to buy, but because they are unable to get loans in the traditional way they are dropping out of the market. This is causing the market to fall even further than it would without this issue.

Seller financing can allow these buyers to buy and help *restore equilibrium* to the market. Therefore I had to write this book. This information needed to be spread to a wider audience than just my seminar students. Unfortunately at one point I had to stop writing. Let me explain.

My students around the country and I are constantly coming up with new ideas to use on deals. It is virtually impossible to keep up with all of the ideas. That is because as you will soon find out, seller financing is truly an unlimited tool for investors! Therefore, in addition to this book I have a 3-day camp where I teach advanced seller financing techniques. I know you will find the information in this book extremely valuable. I also know that I give you *everything* you need to go do incredible deals using seller financing. However, if after reading this book you wish to have even more recent and cutting edge seller financing ideas I invite you to join us at one of these events.

FREE EVENT TICKETS

I am so motivated to help you be a success that my first book comes with 2 FREE tickets one of my upcoming "Super Camps"! These camps are an amazing opportunity to meet fellow investors, and get hands-on training. There is no better way to jump start your investing success than to attend a live MWI event. I hope to see you there!

HOW IS
THE "HIGHEST
AND BEST" USE
RELATED TO
SELLER FINANCING?

HOW IS THE "HIGHEST AND BEST" USE RELATED TO SELLER FINANCING?

It might be confusing if I didn't take a moment and explain a bit more about the basis of "The Foundation to Success". I mentioned briefly that the whole point is to find properties that are not being used for their "Highest and Best" use. Once you find a property that is not currently at its "Highest and Best" use then you can do something to it to make it more valuable.

But how do you make a property worth more money? The way that I determine if a property has a higher and better use is if it is not at its highest *density* as it sits right now.

Density - In real estate, density is the term for the number, compactness, or size of units that an investor can put on a particular project based on the size of the lot and the controlling development standards in the municipality. For Mike Watson Investing (MWI) purposes it also includes the amount of net income the property produces, the number of owners, square footage and terms of a deal.

Definition

There are five different types of density you need to examine to see if there is some room for improvement (i.e. higher profit or more equity position). The first thing that must be done is to look at the *number of units* the property currently has. For instance, let's say you find a single family home on a lot and the zoning of this lot actually permits the building of an apartment complex. Obviously there is a higher and better use for the property in the form of more units.

The second type of density to examine is *square footage*. In other words is there a lot containing a warehouse whose square footage could be increased? If so, this would increase the value of that property. Especially if it is in an area where warehouses are expensive to buy or rent.

The third type of density relates to how many *tax ID* numbers there are on a property. For instance, let's say there is a 4-unit building on a lot in a nice area and there is one owner who rents out all of the units. If you do a condominium conversion on the property you would essentially increase the *number of owners* to 4 thus increasing the amount of tax ID numbers on the same property. This will increase the value of a property dramatically.

The fourth type of density I teach is the amount of *income* that a property generates. I consider cash flow a form of density. In other words, the more positive cash flow a property provides the *denser* it is. There are over 25 ways to increase the cash flow of a property that I discuss in my book "The Highest and Best Real Estate Investment" and they are just some of the basic ideas to get you started. The concept is to increase income and/or decrease expenses thus increasing the density of the cash flow of the property.

The final type of density is *terms*. Terms are the details of the transaction that are negotiated between the buyer and seller. I show you how to manipulate the terms of a deal to increase the value of the property. How is that possible? As an example, if you bought a property with no down payment and walked away from the closing owning a property with positive cash flow, would you care what the *price* was? Or, would it make a difference if you could avoid bringing $200,000 to the closing table? I (and most appraisers) believe it makes a difference in the value of the property. You actually change the value of a property when you change the *terms* of the deal.

Terms - The parts of a loan or contract that help determine all of the agreed upon details. Examples would be interest rate, years in the loan, down payment required and closing costs.

Definition

This book "How to Buy and Sell Real Estate without Using a Bank" is a user's guide on how to manipulate terms in ways most people have never heard. It is the ultimate text on how to use different types of seller financing to make any deal work better for both the buyer *and* the seller.

Seller financing is the most powerful way to unlock your potential for successful investing. This is because in most cases, if you have funds to cover any necessary expenses, you most likely can make a deal work. Seller financing is the most incredible method for raising funds I have ever come across.

Yes, you read that right, I said *raising funds*. Seller financing is a great way to raise private capital for your deals. In addition to teaching you how to raise this capital, my method teaches you how to use this same capital over and over again in the future on many more deals!

Another side effect of seller financing is that it is a fantastic way to get very low price cash offers accepted. I know that sounds unrealistic but I will go over this aspect in great detail when I teach you the "4-offer spreadsheet" technique.

In addition, seller financing will give you ways to sell properties faster and for higher prices than you could if you only offered traditional financing. It will help you sell a property that would otherwise be difficult to sell. These things are true because seller financing increases the number of able buyers, thus demand, which then increases the possibility of a sale and a better price.

Seller financing is also a spectacular way to create passive cash flow when you *sell* a property. This may be the most overlooked benefit of seller financing. When you sell a property and offer seller financing you will have passive income from the financing you offer. Because of this I believe *seller financing is better for the seller than it is for the buyer.* I explore this idea very deeply in the following chapters.

Finally, I intend to expand your idea of wealth. Instead of evaluating a deal based on its full potential most people only look at the short -term profits that can be made. Real estate can be a fantastic vehicle to help you create profits. The only difference is that it is also vital to consider your investment as a vehicle to great *wealth.* I like to include *equity* in property, *cash flows* from income properties, and *income* from notes receivable's as part of the full equation for great wealth.

You will learn how this "great wealth" can be achieved by using seller financing. Seller financing has the capability of creating all of the types of wealth; profits, equity, cash flow from income properties and income from notes receivables. Because of this, I believe it is the "Highest and Best" real estate *tool* for any investor.

Seller financing and the related tools presented here have widespread value for anyone who buys or sells any type of real estate. For that matter you could even apply them to other types of saleable property such as cars, boats recreational vehicles, etc. Honestly you can seller finance *anything.*

You will get to explore the world of seller financing as you have never before experienced it. I would like to invite you to keep an *open mind* as you read. Have fun and partake of this fountain of knowledge. My final invitation for you is to complete a deal so you can reap all of the benefits of seller financing as soon as possible.

CHAPTER **2**

OPEN YOUR MIND TO THE POSSIBILITIES!

OPEN YOUR MIND TO THE POSSIBILITIES!

When was the last time you bought a property and did not use a single penny of your own money to buy it? When was the last time you sold a property and then immediately after you sold it you started *receiving* cash flow from that same property? Let me share with you a mind-bending concept. These two possibilities are only the tip of the iceberg when you explore the power and flexibility of seller financing.

Buying and selling real estate can be as difficult or as easy as you make it. I'm here to help you make it much, much easier. These advanced seller financing techniques are going to show you the secrets of how the mega-millionaires of real estate empires complete deal, after deal, after deal. In fact the bigger the deal the more likely you are to use seller financing. Seller financing is commonly used and accepted on larger deals and with wealthier sellers and buyers.

You will learn exactly how to buy any piece of property and sell any piece of property without the hassles of getting a traditional loan. It doesn't matter what the market is doing or where you live. These concepts work anywhere, and anytime. It is vital to mention here that in a "bad" (Buyer's) market sellers are *more* willing to use these techniques. Use that to your advantage!

A few years ago I was in hot pursuit of my first few millions by investing in real estate. I was finding deals, making profits and creating huge equity positions on properties for my long term portfolio. During that time I learned some valuable techniques that are not commonly used by investors, buyers or sellers, namely, seller financing. During these deals I began to realize that seller financing is better for the *seller* than it is for the buyer.

Yes, you read that right. You might even want to read it again. This idea alone will transform your ability to buy *and* sell anything. This concept is something that no lender in the world wants you to know. Why not? The answer is because it will make lenders obsolete.

This idea of seller financing being better for the seller than it is for the buyer frees you to maximize the massive impact you can have by investing in real estate. This is often a difficult thing for investors to imagine. Usually they only look at a deal from the buyer's side as it applies to seller financing.

Many sellers only consider using seller financing as a "last resort". I, on the other hand, have sold hundreds of properties and offered seller financing to many of those buyers. Because of this I know firsthand how incredible it is to have passive income on the notes month after month and not have to worry about maintenance or management!

Imagine going to an owner of a 12 unit condo complex and being able to negotiate a deal where you do not have to get a bank loan or come up with any money to buy the property. Imagine that seller being *thrilled* at closing. Now, think about how it would feel leaving that closing table owning a 12 unit condo complex that throws positive cash flow to you every month. That is exactly what I did by using seller financing and *so can you*.

When you begin to understand why seller financing is such a profitable proposition for a seller and start to trust and believe in it, you will be able to convince *any* seller to seller finance their property. The funny thing about this process is that not only will you want to *buy* properties using seller financing you will also end up wanting to offer seller financing when you *sell* your properties.

> *The more you learn to think like the seller when it comes to seller financing, the more you will want to BE the seller!*
>
> **~Mike Watson**

The key is to understand the value of seller financing for both parties. And believe me, there are some incredible benefits. I will be going into these benefits in great detail. Once you believe seller financing is the tool that sets investors free then all you have to do is learn the different terms which can be negotiated and how they all fit together for each transaction.

I will also teach you how to create a win/win deal every time you buy or sell real estate. Seller financing is the pinnacle of *all* real estate investing. It is the path to great wealth for all parties involved. Keep reading and we will delve into this truth that seller financing is better for the seller than it is for the buyer. Here is what happened to me:

A few years ago I went to the owner of a 12 unit condo complex that was for sale. The owner had the property for sale for cash only. I had no desire to pay cash. Using large amounts of cash in a deal will tie up a lot of leverage for other investments. I knew there must be some way to make the deal work for both of us without my having to come to the closing with 100% cash. Here is how I found the answer. I asked him, "Why do you want me to pay cash for the property?"

The funny thing is that at the time I didn't really know why I was asking him the question. In a way I was just making small talk and trying to buy some time to think. His answer sparked an idea that has led to incredible profits for me and many others.

He said, "I want to take my proceeds and invest them so I have retirement income. I'm not sure how to do that but I know for sure I am finished with having to manage property". At first that seemed like a perfectly logical answer. But then my mind started kicking it around a bit and here is what happened. My first thought was, why in the world is he getting out of real estate? Why doesn't he just hire a property manager and keep his asset? What is he thinking?

The truth is, he was burned out on management and was the type of person who was unable or unwilling to hand over control to another person or company. This issue resulted in a deal that worked for both of us. My mind started going over the possibilities. I said to him, "What if there was a way for you to have the income you want even if I don't pay you cash for your property?"

He looked a little confused so I continued. I said, "Why don't you just finance the property for me and I'll pay you an interest rate higher than your bank or broker? That way you will not have to *own* the property anymore but you will still get passive income." He looked at me with a bit of apprehension and said, "Well, I *really* don't want to manage anymore and I don't want to get the property back to have to resell again later. What can you do to guarantee that?"

I understood his concern (that I wouldn't pay him) and decided to be straight-forward with him. I told him, "There is no way you are going to get this property back. The property is going to be a retirement plan for me and my family. I am never going to let you have it back."

You might think that it was risky saying this. That he might see what he was giving up by selling to me. But the truth was he did not want the property anymore. He wanted to sell. All he wanted was an assurance that I was not going to make his life harder than it already was. He wanted to know I was going to make all of my payments. The funny thing is that the *property* was going to be making the payments.

After a bit more discussion he agreed to finance the *entire* purchase price to me. (Later I'll give you some great tips for this part of the negotiations.) He saw the light and wanted to get as much passive cash flow as he could by giving me the largest loan possible.

He realized that by letting me have a note for the entire part of his equity he would have the most amount of income possible. He understood that more cash down literally meant less income for him each month. He didn't want the cash, he wanted the *income*.

Income was the reason he owned the building in the first place. Most people who own rental or investment property understand this fundamental issue. They think property management is a necessary evil to earn their residual income. Imagine how excited people will become when they understand they can have cash flow with no property management!

On top of the cash flow, another benefit was that he did not have to pay a huge amount of tax that year and then risk what was left of his profits on an unsure investment. Instead he financed the property to me and immediately started to receive nice interest checks every month without having to do any more management. In addition he postponed his tax burden to the years when he would receive his principle. We were both very happy. Truth be told, I was happy and he was ecstatic!

This transaction changed my views on seller financing. When I started using seller financing I had no idea how powerful it was for both of the parties in the transaction. I have since learned that there is no other technique available in real estate investing that is better than seller financing for making deals work. It frees all parties to achieve exactly what they need in order to profit.

Seller financing gives the seller *passive income* without property management. If you use seller financing when you sell you will watch your passive income soar. It also lets a buyer purchase *any* property. When you learn how to get seller financing on any transaction, your buying power goes up exponentially over-night.

Seller financing has the power to revolutionize the real estate world by freeing both buyers and sellers. When you completely understand this concept, I hope you will choose to yield the sword of freedom within the investing arena.

Finally, remember, that in order to make seller financing work you only have to do two things. First, you need to *intimately* know the seller financing terms you will use to create a winning transaction for all parties. This is important so you can put together deals that will work. Second, you must understand how seller financing is better for the seller than it is for the buyer. You need to believe this so deeply that when you talk with sellers this truth will convince them of the value of the transaction and they will become as excited as you are.

Now, let's explore the basics of the first item.

WHAT IS
SELLER FINANCING?

CHAPTER **3**

WHAT IS
SELLER FINANCING?

What is seller financing?

> **Seller Financing** - Financing that the seller offers to buyers as a part of
> the sale of their property. Using seller financing, the seller then becomes
> the bank for part or all of the buyer's purchase. Terms are agreed upon
> by both parties and a mortgage is created at the property closing.
>
> Definition

The bottom line is this, seller financing takes place when the *seller is the bank for the buyer*. That's it! You don't have to understand anything else at this point. I'll eventually give you many fantastic ways to use this tool but for now just understand how simple seller financing really is.

Why is this simple tool so powerful? Why do I feel an entire book is needed for this topic alone? Why is it important enough to expend a lot of time teaching these different techniques? The answer to all of these questions is, seller financing makes it possible for anyone to buy anything and anyone to sell anything.

Read that again. Isn't this what everyone is searching for in real estate? If you can buy any property you want and then sell it you have the ability to be an investor. This may seem obvious but look at it a little closer.

What usually stops people from investing? Normally the answer is money. Either they don't have any extra money or they can't qualify for a loan at a traditional bank or mortgage company. (Or they can't make the terms of the deal work to create a profit). If they don't need their own money to buy a property and a profit can be made by manipulating the terms of the sale, then nothing stands in their way?

Another concern for buyers is, "What if I can't sell the property after I buy it?" This issue can also be handled with seller financing. When you offer the right kind of seller financing to buyers you create your own market niche. Imagine what kind of interest there would be in your properties if they came with their own financing that practically anyone could qualify for. Your phone would ring off the hook with interested parties!

Thanks to some truly doubtful lending practices over the last few years, and the resulting backlash from those practices, there is now a gigantic demand for financing that is not being met by traditional lenders. If you are able to pick up just a tiny bit of that slack, you will profit handsomely.

How could seller financing change the investing and/or real estate world if it were widely taught and understood? Would there be fewer foreclosures? Would there be more opportunities for investors to realize financial gain from buying real estate? Would it be easier to buy properties even though traditional lending institutions were making getting a loan more difficult? I believe it would do all of these things and more. Our nation would greatly benefit by buyers and sellers using these techniques. Learn seller financing and then help yourself and others by utilizing this information.

During one of my "Highest and Best" Boot Camps an attendee stood up in front of the class on the first day and said, "I totally understand how your investing system has the potential to change the world for the better. I see that investing can help many people including, but not limited to, the seller, the buyer, the contractors, the investors and the neighborhoods. But here is my problem, I don't have any money. How am I supposed to buy deals?"

I looked at her and said, "Hold on tight. You're in for a wild ride!" Since I hadn't gotten to the section on seller financing yet she had to wait until the following morning to find out what I meant. The next day after I finished that section I turned and asked her, "What do you think now?"

She stood up and said, "I wouldn't have believed it was true. Yesterday I didn't think I could do these types of deals. Today I know with absolute certainty that I can." I had given her an entirely new way to think about investing. She had discovered the limitless possibilities for profits and cash flows that seller financing provides.

She saw the light. She really felt the power of seller financing. She knew that with the tools I was giving her she did not need to have cash to buy and sell real estate. She also knew that she could sell *any* property. This was a huge relief for her as it is for most people who understand the power of seller financing.

Let me tell you a story about another one of my students. She had been a real estate investor for 15 years when she came to my "Highest and Best" boot camp. She had done lots of investments over the years but had never used seller financing or closed on a property without bringing money to the table.

Because of her backgroundI know she grasped the concepts I taught. For five months she came to seminars and even bought one property that was going to be a very lucrative deal. Then she went to my "Advanced Seller Financing" Degree Camp.

All during the Camp she kept asking questions and clarifying the information. It was obvious she was excited about the possibility of actually using the techniques discussed in that Camp. Six months later I spoke with her and she had bought three additional properties using "The Foundation to Success". She had negotiated seller financing on every single one of them and had also given zero down payment on all of them. She told me that after the camp she had finally understood why seller financing was such a wonderful opportunity for both the buyer and the seller. In addition, she also had all the tools to implement seller financing.

This book will cover almost everything I teach in my "Advanced Seller Financing" Degree Camp (I keep updating my live Camps). If you read "The Highest and Best Real Estate Investment" and this book you will be armed with the most powerful investing techniques available in the market today. This I guarantee.

Seller financing is vital to your investing career. Without it you are like a baby learning to crawl. With it you are running in the Olympics! It has the power to take any investor from being a beginner to an advanced investor in a very short time. In addition, if you are a seasoned investor and are not using seller financing on a normal basis this will skyrocket your efforts and results. Seller financing completely opens up your options. Remember, it allows you to buy *any* property and sell *any* property. Imagine the possibilities!

Imagine what it would be like to buy as many properties as you want and never have to ask a bank or mortgage company for their permission or funds ever again. Imagine the freedom this will bring to your investing. Your job while reading this book is to expand your mind.

 Seller financing is the holy grail of real estate investing!

~Mike Watson

FREE Online Resources

To see examples of seller financing in action, go to the MWI Forum on my website at **www.mikewatsoninvesting.com** and look at the section of the Forum called "It Works". You will see student after student who is profiting by using these ideas!

SELLER FINANCING IS BETTER FOR THE SELLER THAN IT IS FOR THE BUYER

SELLER FINANCING IS BETTER FOR THE SELLER THAN IT IS FOR THE BUYER

Before I get into the finer details of seller financing I want to review why it is imperative to understand how seller financing is *better for the seller* than it is for the buyer. The main reason is this; if you believe it is true then you can convey the idea to *others* effectively. This means you will be able to talk to anyone about any deal and convince them that seller financing is a great deal for everyone. (Which it is!)

Your true understanding of the capability of seller financing is the first step in being able to negotiate seller financing on any property. With your understanding, heartfelt belief, and the tools you'll learn, you will be unstoppable in real estate investing!

Let's move on to why seller financing is so good for all parties of a transaction. Let's first investigate the many reasons why seller financing is good for the buyer. These reasons include but are not limited to the following;

Benefits for the Buyer

1. ALL buyers qualify! There are no standard qualifications. The seller may ask for something to feel more comfortable but

usually these things are minimal. In one case a seller just wanted the buyer to disclose that the buyer had previously owned another property and had made all the payments.

2. It is *easy* to close. You don't have to get appraisals, surveys, inspections etc. In some cases you may still *want* to get these things but they are not required.

3. The buyers don't have to go through the typical red tape involved with getting a loan through a bank or mortgage company. In other words they don't have to provide all of the following items and more: proof of income, bank statements, tax returns, all investment data, all corporate information, credit reports etc.

4. Closings can occur very *quickly*. The main thing requiring time is getting a title policy. On some properties you can get a title policy in two or three days. This is much faster than getting a loan with a traditional lender where you have to do an appraisal, inspections, survey, loan approval etc. These things can take months.

Title Policy - A contract of indemnity issued to the owner of a piece of property guaranteeing a "free and clear" title up to the face amount of the title policy. Should any previous claims arise against the title of a property; the title insurance policy will take care of those claims.

Definition

5. There is *no mortgage insurance required*. This can potentially save you thousands of dollars at closing and over the life of
the loan.

> **Mortgage Insurance** – A fee that a lender will typically charge if
> you do not put at least 20% as a down payment. This fee is paid to a
> company that insures the lender will be paid on the loan even if you do
> not pay your mortgage.
>
> Definition

6. Sometimes sellers will sell *because* you let them seller finance
They understand the benefits and would prefer to finance their
equity and receive interest on it. They like cash flow without
maintenance.

7. The closing costs are low. There are no lender's fees, points etc.

> **Point** - A fee usually equal to one percent of the loan amount in a real
> estate transaction. This fee is usually charged in association with the
> creation of a loan.
>
> Definition

8. It is possible to invest with little or *no money down*. You can
negotiate any terms you like so why not ask the seller to allow
you to put just a small amount or no money down? If you combine
the different types of seller financing you can accomplish this on
almost every purchase.

9. You can negotiate all of the terms with the seller, unlike with
a bank. You could end up paying zero interest or not having to

make payments for several years. You might even negotiate so you don't have to pay off the full amount of the loan. (Keep reading, this is a fun one)

Terms - The parts of a loan or contract that help determine all of the agreed upon details. Examples would be interest rate, years in the loan, down payment required and closing costs.

Definition

10. You can re-sell the property easier if the seller finance loan is a simple assumption. If the seller agrees to allow the loan to be a simple assumption then in essence it is a non-qualifying loan for the next buyer. This can create *more value* (that is, higher profits) in the property and an easier sale for you.

11. You can use more of your attention on your evaluation of the merits of the property rather than on the mind numbing details of getting a loan.

Many people have heard of some of these benefits for buyers, but most traditional investors do not understand why seller financing is better for the *seller*. Most people think that the buyer is the only one getting any advantages when seller financing is used. This is just not the case.

In most cases when properties are sold, the sellers take their proceeds from the sale, pay taxes, and spend or save the balance. How have these actions improved the sellers' current and future wealth? How have they improved their lives? Maybe they don't have to manage the property anymore. Maybe they have cash in their pocket? But let's examine this a little closer.

When sellers take their equity out as profits they have not improved their position at all. They have simply traded equity for cash. That is, previously they had equity in the property, now they have cash.

In most cases the sellers will have to pay taxes on their profits which lowers the amount of cash they have. This means they have *less cash* than they used to have in *equity in their property*. The net effect is they are in a worse position as far as net worth, than they were when they owned the property.

> **Net worth** – A person's financial position when you subtract all of their liabilities from their assets.
>
> Definition

Let me give you a quick example. Let's say you own an apartment with a loan on it for $500,000 and you sell it for $1,000,000. One would think that would create a gain of $500,000.

However, we will assume you paid $600,000 for it 5 years ago and put down $100,000. That means you currently have *equity* of $500,000 and you had a *gain* of $400,000.

If you sell the property and keep the proceeds you will most likely have to pay closing costs in excess of $50,000 plus capital gains and recapture taxes anywhere between $60,000 and $100,000 or even more. This means that you will only end up with a gain of about $250,000. That is *half* of your net worth compared to when you *owned* the property!

The worst part about all of this is now you have a lump sum of cash you have to do something with, and no more residual income. I equate this outcome with financially falling on your own sword.

The only way to increase your own net worth and cash flow when you sell a property is by turning around and investing the proceeds from the sale. What is the easiest way to invest those funds? Is it in stocks, mutual funds, or another property? Who can really tell? These are all just guessing games.

Most people who are selling income producing real estate do not want to buy more income producing real estate. They are getting out because they don't want to manage anymore. When you buy a home from someone they will usually be buying another home to live in or will be taking the money and perhaps spending or saving it.

The better option, in both of these situations, is seller financing. If you can show the seller how to *increase their net worth* and their passive cash flow the day they close, you are doing them a huge favor. Let's go over how this works.

Using the example above let's say that instead of selling your $1,000,000 apartment complex outright you agree to seller finance your *equity*. This means your buyer must get a loan or bring enough cash to the closing to pay off your existing loan and closing costs. So, in this example they bring $550,000 to closing. Next you as the seller, give them a loan for the $450,000 (the balance of your equity). This way you still retain the lion's share of your equity and receive continued cash flows based on that higher amount!

In other words, had you sold the property outright and paid your tax burden you would have $250,000 to invest. If you seller finance you can "invest" $450,000 at a great interest rate with that buyer.

Here is what else happens when you offer seller financing. First you no longer have to handle any property management. Second you get passive income. Third, you only have to pay capital gains taxes on the principal part of the loan you receive each year. And finally your net worth goes up.

You now possess a note payable for $450,000 *plus* interest owed to you by the note holder. If you gave them a 5-year loan and they are paying 8% your net worth is now $630,000. ($450,000 *principal* owed plus $180,000 of *interest* owed) I'd say seller financing has put you in an awesome situation. Instead of your net worth being $250,000 it is $630,000!

Now let's take a look at some of the other benefits that the sellers enjoy when they offer seller financing to a buyer.

Benefits to the Seller:

1. Your closing can happen very *fast*. Basically, all that is needed is a title policy and a review of the buyer's financial capabilities.

2. Seller financing can provide you cash at closing *plus* income over time.

3. Your capital gains taxes can be spread over time since all proceeds won't be claimed or received in one year. You may not even have capital gains until the *end* of the loan if you are receiving "interest only" payments. (Check with your CPA)

4. *All buyers qualify!* This creates more demand for your property and thus you can sell it faster and for a higher price. Even *fantastic* buyers prefer seller financing to the hassle caused by having to get a new loan from a bank or mortgage company. (I certainly do.)

5. If the property has to be reclaimed, property values may have increased plus you will have made money during the time you were receiving loan payments.

6. It is easier to sell the property - even one that may be otherwise difficult to sell.

7. You can make a *higher return* on your money when you loan it to the buyer than you could on other investments such as a money market, interest bearing bank account or CD.

8. You have *no property management* even though you have cash flow. I like to call this property-less passive income. In many cases the cash flow from the seller financing is *more* than your previous net rental income. (This is especially possible when a

buyer will be changing the use of your property into a "Higher and Better" use.)

I would imagine you are starting to realize why seller financing can make or break a deal. No, actually at this point I would think you are starting to say to yourself, "The benefits of seller financing are ASTOUNDING! I have to do it!" If you are thinking this, you are well on your way to creating great wealth for yourself and others.

> *Seller financing is the ultimate tool in real estate investing because it is the most flexible type of buying and selling power that exists.*
>
> **~Mike Watson**

Real Life Seller Financing Example:

A couple of my students found a great cash flowing 30 unit apartment complex with a much "Higher and Better" use. (The income "density" could be increased significantly.) The students made an offer using a "4-offer spreadsheet". (See Chapter 17)

The highest offer they made was for $795,000. In this offer they asked for 100% seller financing. Their lowest offer was for $710,000 and was for cash. The seller accepted the lower offer to get the cash.

My students insisted the seller be at the walk-through inspection on the property. After much discussion about the building, they asked the seller if they could talk about the sale. He agreed and they said, "What are you planning on doing with your proceeds?" He said, "I am going to pay off my loan, buy a boat and sail up the Mississippi River from the Gulf of Mexico to St. Louis for a year. I'll use the rest of the proceeds to live on for a few years."

When they heard this, my students told him they couldn't believe he didn't take the seller financing offer. They showed him how it would have allowed him to get cash to pay off his small remaining mortgage and how it would have financed his trip.

They explained how his equity would earn property-less passive income when left as a loan to the buyer. This equity would produce a monthly interest income that would pay him more than his boat payment *plus* pay for his monthly needs. On top of that his entire principal would be unused when he got back from his trip.

They suggested he use the first seven years worth of payments on a 10-year interest-only loan for $250,000 (*part* of his equity position) to finance his boat and trip and then *pay off* his boat. He would then receive three more years of interest income and still be owed his $250,000 at the end of the ten years. Then he could sail around the world!

The seller still wasn't sure what to do. My students helped him out in his decision-making process. After seeing the building and the other deals on the market at that time, they decided it didn't make sense to give one seller $710,000 in cash when that same cash could be used as multiple down payments for multiple purchases.

They called the seller's agent and said they were backing out. They said, "It doesn't make sense for us to use up that much of our cash. We are going to back out before due diligence is over."

The seller's agent quickly asked my students, "Is the seller financing option still on the table?" They told him it was.

They expected the seller's agent to send over an addendum changing the sale from a $710,000 cash deal to a $795,000 seller financing deal. This was based on their original "4-offer spreadsheet" numbers.

To their surprise they seller came back at $710,000 (The *cash* price) with $300,000 cash down and *$410,000* of seller financing for one year. (He has since extended this financing for two more years.)

My students were elated. Not only did they get the seller financing they asked for but they also got it at the cash price. The funny thing is that the seller was happy too. All of the parties understood how this method was really going to benefit them.

Are you beginning to understand what an incredible deal this was for the seller? Are you now getting an idea how powerful seller financing is?

Why was the seller now very happy to offer seller financing when the day before it was being refused? *Here is the key: The seller's mind was changed because the students believed in the virtues of seller financing and exposed its true value to the seller.* They showed the seller how the same goals could be achieved, but in a much better way for both the buyer and the seller. The seller received the cash he needed up front and the passive income he needed for the future. In addition the seller did not have to manage the property anymore!

Now, let's talk a little bit about the final benefit for the seller. How did offering seller financing increase the seller's net worth? Let's assume the seller's net worth was his net equity in the property. ($410,000) If the seller takes the profits of the sale in cash there is no improvement to his net worth. This is because he is just trading the equity he had in the property, which was a part of his net worth, for cash. As a matter of fact if he took the profits as cash his net worth actually goes *down*. Whereas before he had all of the equity in the property, now he has to pay taxes on his gain.

For instance, if he had to pay 20% in taxes on the $410,000 gain ($82,000) he would now have a net worth of only $328,000.

Instead, let's look at what happened when the seller gave the students $410,000 worth of financing at 10%. His net worth went *up* because he now had the seller financing note due to him for $410,000 plus the *interest* due on the note. If the note is for five years and he receives $41,000 per year in interest the seller is now worth $205,000 ($41,000 x 5) *more* than he was before he sold the property!

- Net worth when owning property $410,000
- Net worth when sell property and take cash $328,000 (Equity $410,000 - $82,000 tax burden)
- Net worth when sell and seller finance equity $615,000! (Equity $410,000 plus interest owed $205,000)

SELLER FINANCING EXAMPLE

Net Worth

Owns property

$410,000 Equity   **= $410,000**

Sold Outright

$328,000 Net equity	Taxes, closing costs, etc

= $328,000

Sold with Seller Financing

$410,000 Equity	$205,000 Interest owed

= $615,000

Here is an interesting addendum to this particular deal. After the seller agreed to seller finance to the students, they put together a new contract with the terms of the seller financing that the seller had agreed on.

The day after they gave the new contract to the seller's agent they got a phone call from him. The agent said, "You must have made a mistake with the contract." At first the students felt a little anxious that the seller might have changed his mind but they held their tongue and listened. The agent continued, "The seller does not want to be paid the interest every month. He only wants you to pay the payments *yearly* so he doesn't have to worry about the checks each month while he is gone on his boat. You can *start in one year.*"

As you can imagine this was quite a pleasant surprise for my students. Now, not only did they not have to qualify for the full traditional commercial financing but they also had no payments on over half of the purchase price of the property for an entire year!

My students are now putting their net rental profits into an interest bearing savings account and are going to use that interest to help pay their interest payment to the seller in one year. They are actually *profiting* from not having to make monthly payments. Every little bit helps, especially when working with larger numbers.

Seller financing makes it easier and maybe even less expensive for a buyer to purchase a property, but the true value lies with the *seller*. When a seller finances the property and only collects interest payments, capital gains taxes are delayed. In addition the seller is released from the burden of property management, yet at the same time cash flow and net worth are increased!

> *Seller financing is better for the seller than it is for the buyer.*
>
> **~Mike Watson**

CHAPTER **5**

ISN'T SELLER FINANCING RISKY?

ISN'T SELLER FINANCING RISKY?

By now you may be getting excited about how you personally can use seller financing. On the other hand you may still have some doubts. Or, you may have told someone about the technique and gotten negative responses such as, "Seller financing is risky." or "I knew someone who seller financed and they ended up having to take the property back." They might even have said, "There is no way I'd ever seller finance anything." The truth is that most of these people do not understand the benefits of seller financing as you soon will.

Hopefully you are keeping that "open mind" we talked about earlier. I will explain to you right now when seller financing is risky and also when it is not. First let's talk about the buyer's risk. Let's assume you are the buyer. When would it be risky for you to get seller financing from a seller?

There are three times when it would be risky. The first would be when you pay the sellers directly and they have extended you blanket financing, also known as a wrap. Blanket financing is when sellers have a loan on the property and they finance the property for you without paying off their loan. They "wrap" their loan to you over their existing loan. What happens is you make a payment to the seller, then they turn around and pay that other loan each time a payment is due.

In this case the risk is if you make your payments directly to the sellers and *they* don't make that underlying loan payment. Then *you* could lose the property. That other lender could foreclose even if you've made every payment in full and on time to the seller. We will address this situation at length in the section on "The Rules of Wrapping". There are ways to make this much less risky.

The second risk is if the sellers have a government loan on the property. (FHA, VA, etc.) In this case you should never incorporate the "Blanket" (or wrap) technique. There are penalties for financing "over" this type of loan. Regular conventional and commercial loans may have penalties to the sellers if they sell and allow the loan to be wrapped. Government loans can also have penalties for the *buyer*. (Most title companies will not even close this type of transaction as they can lose their right to insure if they do.)

The third time it is risky to do seller financing is when you are the buyer and the sellers agree to allow you to wrap their loan and it has a "Due on Sale Clause".

> **Due on Sale Clause** – This is a clause that is sometimes in a loan that states the loan is due and payable or can be called due and payable at the time the property is sold.
>
> Definition

This may cause a problem because even if the seller pays the loan religiously the "Due on Sale Clause" may have been violated by selling you the property and not first paying off the loan. The bank then has the right to ask for the loan to be paid in full immediately.

Fortunately I am going to teach you a way to mitigate this risk or remove this clause entirely from the loan documents. In tough times such as in 2009, the last thing a bank wants to do is foreclose on a mortgage that is being paid on time and in full. If you follow my instructions in a later chapter, the issue of the "Due on Sale Clause" can be completely overcome.

What I want you to notice is all of these risky issues only occur when there is another loan on the property and you "Wrap or Blanket" that loan. In other words, if you stay away from that type of seller financing there is not much risk. That is unless you don't plan on paying the payments to the seller or the taxes on the property. This of course could lead to foreclosure by the seller or county treasurer. Keep in mind those risks are inherent in owning any property with *any* type of financing attached to it. We will always assume this is not your plan.

Now let's explore the possible risk for the seller. Imagine you are the seller and a buyer is asking you to seller finance to him. This is usually what people are talking about when they say, "Seller financing is risky." They are inferring that you are taking a huge risk with that particular buyer. That may be true if you do not follow this advice. Always qualify your buyer, get a down payment and, *only seller finance your equity*. Let's examine these three things a little closer.

First and foremost, always qualify your buyers! That doesn't mean you hold them to the stringent standards of a traditional lender. It does mean you check their credit report and make sure they don't have a lot of "bad" credit. This would also include making sure they do not have an overly burdensome amount of debt based on their income. It also means you verify their income to ensure it is sufficient to make the payments. I don't let anyone buy a property from me who doesn't make a monthly salary 3-4 times the amount of the full payment of the property (including tax and insurance).

In addition it is always smart to get some sort of a down payment. The larger the down payment you get the lower risk you have in the property. However, a larger down payment also means the amount of seller financing you can offer will be lower thus your monthly income from the loan will be less. All of these things are tied together and need to be carefully considered in each situation.

As far as the buyer is concerned, typically the lower the amount of the down payment, the higher the price can be and vice versa. Therefore, you may not want to ask for too much of a down payment if your potential buyer is very price sensitive. These are just some suggestions. You, of course will make your own determinations as to what kind of risks you are willing to take with each buyer.

Finally, if the issues mentioned are not all to your satisfaction you might consider having the buyer get a co-signer on the loan. That way if the buyer defaults then you have another person to collect from before you have to start foreclosure proceedings to take your property back.

The most important thing to remember when it comes to risk is this, if you own a property and want to enjoy the tremendous benefits of offering seller financing to a buyer without much risk then *only finance your equity or profits.*

For instance, if you own a property and it is worth $600,000 and you have a loan on it for $200,000 then you should only offer to seller finance the underlying remaining $400,000. (This is your equity.) That way when you sell the property the loan is paid off and you are only risking your *profits*. Conversely, if you seller finance a property on which you still owe a loan and the buyer quits paying, you will still have a mortgage payment even though you don't own the property anymore. This can be quite painful.

If you are only risking your profits you have essentially lowered your true risk down to zero. If the worst case scenario occurred you could take the property back and re-sell it and most likely make your original profit or possibly more.

As a seller you want to always collateralize the note you make with the property. You want to be in the first lien position if there is no other lien. You want to be in the second lien position if the buyers obtained their own first lien. Finally you must make sure that all liens on the property are a lower amount than the value of the property.

We will talk about these issues in great detail. For now remember this: *seller financing is only risky when you finance more than your equity.*

Now let's move on to the basic methods you can use to seller finance properties.

9 WAYS TO SELLER FINANCE PROPERTIES

9 WAYS TO SELLER FINANCE PROPERTIES

A few months ago I was teaching one of my "Advanced Seller Financing" Degree Camps and a student raised her hand. When I called on her, she said, "I'm starting to think that there are unlimited ways to seller finance a property." I chuckled and replied, "Then you are beginning to understand seller financing."

Seller financing is literally *unlimited* in its options and potential. When the seller is the source of the financing then the buyer and seller can quite literally negotiate *any* terms they wish. They can negotiate win/win transactions without banks and bureaucracies getting in the way. This fact alone is the most freeing aspect of purchasing real estate using seller financing.

I will go through as many different techniques in this book as possible but if you attend one of my "Advanced Seller Financing" Degree Camps you will find that I teach even more new techniques that my students and I have uncovered since this material was written.

Seller financing options will continue to grow in number as long as investors have an open mind. Let's get to the basic techniques. These are the fundamental ideas from which you can expand.

1. Free and Clear Seller Financing

This type of seller financing occurs when, as the name implies, the seller owns the property "free and clear". In other words, there are no existing loans on the property. The most fun thing about this type of seller financing (and why it is my favorite type) is that it is 100% unlimited! What do I mean by that? I mean there are *no rules*, barriers, or limitations. This is truly a creative endeavor.

The buyer and the seller can create their financing agreement *any* way they wish. When you get to the Chapter that discusses "The 23 Most Powerful Terms to Negotiate with Seller Financing" you can use *all* of them with this type of seller financing.

In fact, in the chapter on finding amazing seller financing opportunities I will show you some techniques you can use to *find* properties that are owned free and clear.

One of my students recently used one of these techniques and was able to find 616 free and clear properties within two zip codes. Imagine the seller financing opportunities he will have when he contacts these owners. He will be able to easily improve the sellers' returns and most likely their income, too. At the same time he will be able to relieve those who are tired of property management. Many individuals might sell based on these two facts alone.

The other thing I love about free and clear seller financing is it's easy to get sellers a down payment at closing if they want one as part of the sale. Many sellers don't ask for a large down payment because they want to keep their income as high as possible (more on this in a bit). The exciting thing is if they *do* want a down payment you just go to the bank and get a small loan equal to that amount. (Ideally you would also add on closing costs to this loan)

For example if a seller had a million dollar property for sale and wanted a 10% down payment it would be simple to get a $100,000 loan from a bank. The seller will need to allow that $100,000 loan to be the first lien on the property. (The bank will drool to give you this loan as a first lien) This should not be an issue for the seller because the seller will be receiving that $100,000 at closing in cash.

2. Equity-only Seller Financing

Equity-only seller financing is almost as spectacular as the first type. It is where sellers finance their *equity only*. This means they have a loan on the property and will finance everything except the amount of that loan. What the buyer does is get a first lien with a bank to cover the seller's outstanding loan amount (and possibly closing costs and the amount of cash the seller wants at closing). Next the seller gives the buyer a second lien on some or *all of the remainder* of the purchase price.

This technique has become one of my favorites. Here is how it works. I just go to a smaller local bank that does its own loans in-house and get the loan I need. Then I have the seller finance to me the balance of the purchase price. I have done dozens of these types of transactions with my students in the last few years.

Here is an example of one deal where I partnered with a student. She had found a property with a higher and better use. She offered the seller $275,000 for the property. The seller had a loan for $220,000 on the property that needed to be paid off at closing. The student got a loan from the bank for the $220,000 and then the seller financed a loan for the balance of the price. ($55,000) The student then changed the property to its "Higher and Better" use over the next few months, and sold it for $365,000.

The most amazing thing about this type of deal was the student and I went to closing with less than $2000! This is the fastest way to amass a real estate fortune. Find a property with a "Higher and Better" use and then buy it with very little or no money down, change the use and sell it. Or, keep it in your long term portfolio for cash flow. (Do you like to buy properties with no money down as much as I do?)

EQUITY-ONLY SELLER FINANCING EXAMPLE

Purchase Price $275k		
$220k = Buyers new loan that pays off seller's loan	**$55k** = Seller financed portion	**= Zero Down**

3. "Subject To", "Wrap" or "Blanket" Financing

These are all different names for the same type of seller financing. They all mean the seller has a loan on the property and is going to allow the buyer to "wrap" (like a blanket) or assume that loan without consent (in some cases) from the existing mortgage company. The phrase, "subject to", means the buyer is purchasing the property from the seller "subject to" the seller's existing mortgage.

The seller will pass the title to the buyer with a free and clear marketable title "subject to", or except for, the old mortgage which will be "wrapped".

This process can be used when the new buyer does not want, or is unable to get, a new loan for their purchase and there is a current loan on the property.

Here is an example. A seller has a loan on his property for $150,000. There is a willing buyer who agrees to pay the seller $200,000 for the property but cannot quite qualify for a new loan. In this case the seller could ask the buyer to put $50,000 down. The seller would then offer the buyer a new seller financed loan for the remaining $150,000. The seller finance loan payments would cover the payments for the existing loan (which would *not* be paid off at closing). In essence they are "wrapping" the new loan around the old loan.

The mechanism you use to set up this kind of mortgage is called an "All-Inclusive Trust Deed and Note". The "all inclusive" part of the name means your purchase includes the pre-existing loan the seller has on the property. The "trust deed" portion means the seller secures your "wrap" on the title in the form of a "trust deed".

The trust deed is an anchor against the title of a property. The note portion is the terms or the repayment agreement you and the seller negotiate. These terms do not have to be the same as the seller's other note. (But keep them very similar or it could present problems, more on this later.)

There are risks associated with these types of loans. Most existing loans have a "due on sale" clause. The "due on sale" clause is a clause that typically states that if the seller sells the property and does not pay off the original mortgage then the mortgage company has the *right* to call the note due and payable at that time or at any time in the future. (As we spoke of earlier.)

If you want to use this technique make sure you understand the "rules of wrapping" taught in a later section, and verify with a title company and attorney that this is possible in your area. (Or get the mortgage company to remove the "due on sale" clause... keep reading for lots more on this!)

4. Combo Seller Financing

Combo seller financing is simply a combination of the two previous types. In other words the underlying mortgage is "wrapped" *and* some equity is financed by the seller.

This happens when there is a loan on the property but the owner has more equity above the loan and is willing to seller finance that equity. In this case the buyers would not have to get a new loan at all. Neither would they have to come up with the entire amount of the seller's equity as a down payment. They could even do a "zero down" transaction with no qualifying! (Sound familiar?)

So in the example from the last section let's assume the seller said it was OK for the buyer to bring only $20,000 rather than $50,000 to the closing, and then the seller offered a second lien to the buyer for $30,000. The buyer brings $20,000 to the table at closing and gives it to the seller as a down payment. The seller then gives the buyer a $150,000 first lien and a $30,000 second Lien. The buyer makes both payments to the seller and the seller pays the original $150,000 note.

Another intriguing option would be if the buyer did not bring any cash to closing but was given a $150,000 first lien and $50,000 second lien from the seller. But would a seller actually let a buyer come to closing without any money?

Here is the answer, "Yes! Yes! Yes! I see my students accomplish this all the time." A seller *will* allow a buyer to come to the closing with no money because *it increases the seller's cash flow (via higher loan payments) and their net worth as much as possible.* Keep *this* in mind whenever you are negotiating your down payment!

Another great way to use this technique is when sellers have missed some payments. In our current economy there are many sellers who have this problem but who still have equity in their home. What you could do is bring their loan up to good standing so there is no foreclosure and then get a second loan from the seller for the remaining equity. In one transaction you have just helped them save their credit by avoiding foreclosure *and* helped them keep their equity!

5. Purchase Options

In the first four types of seller financing the sellers are acting as the bank *after* closing. In this next scenario the seller is acting as the bank *before* closing. Yes, you read that right. Here is how it works:

When you put down money in order to have the right to buy a property at a fixed price over a certain amount of time that is called a *purchase option.*

For instance, you could purchase an option to buy 1,000 acres, 100 acres at a time over the next ten years. That way you could develop or sell each section over time without having to first purchase the entire 1000 acres. During the "option" time you do some of the initial evaluation and changes to the property (See "Creating and Enhancing Equity in the "Highest and Best" book.) As a result you have *no* loan carrying costs until you actually close on each portion of the property.

Why do I call this seller financing? I consider anything that allows me to have access to a property without getting a new loan on it to be seller financing. In this case the seller is actually paying the carrying costs on the property for you in exchange for your option money. All the while you are doing something to the property which makes it worth more money. The beauty of this is by the time you close on the purchase you will most likely have a new buyer to sell to and some appreciation in the property.

There are a few negatives involved with purchase options. First, they may be *years* in length and in most cases they will require a large deposit. The deposits are typically somewhere between 3-5% of the total future purchase price. Second, if changes need to be made to the property which require you having your name on the title, this option may be somewhat limiting. Third, you are risking time and money on a property that you do not legally own. That said I prefer *purchase contracts* over *purchase options* any day. Let me explain...

6. Extended Closing

An extended closing is similar to the "Purchase Option" except it may not be for such a long period of time and may not require as large a deposit. In addition you are actually filling out an entire *purchase contract* and negotiating an agreement of all terms with the seller. This, in my opinion, is better than a "Purchase Option" because you have more leverage in court to ensure the other party adheres to the contract. All of that is nice but just what is an "Extended Closing", and why is it a type of seller financing?

An "Extended Closing" is where you put a property under contract and do not close on it for an extended amount of time. There are many reasons to do this. One example would be to get a property under contract and have the closing date be 6 months from now. Usually the only cost for the buyer to hold the property during this time is earnest money which will go toward the purchase. So, if you buy the property you essentially have *no* holding costs during those 6 months.

I consider this to be a type of seller financing because during those 6 months you will have *access* to the property to make many of the changes to increase its value without having the added cost of *owning* the property. (For instance, you may be able to start the development, re-zoning or condo-conversion process.) Had you bought the property quickly it would have cost you money to just hold it until those changes were made. You would have had upkeep and loan payments to pay. Instead, it is costing the sellers money. Therefore it is seller financing. They are "carrying the cost of the property" while you enhance its value.

As a caution let me remind you that your name is not on the title so you may not be able to do *some* of the changes. The best way to get some changes started is to ask the seller during negotiations if they will allow you to do so. Have the seller agree and put in writing exactly what you will be allowed to complete prior to closing.

One of the most expensive costs of owning real estate is the monthly debt service. (also known as your loan payments) It is important to minimize this expense as much as possible. The "Extended Closing" is an effective method to do that if you don't need your name on the title to start or complete some or all of the changes. Here are some reasons why a closing could be extended:

1. You need time to get your financing.
2. The property requires physical improvements during the feasibility time.
3. Your due diligence on the property and the conditions take an extended amount of time. (In some cases, such as with larger

developments, this is routine.)

4. The seller doesn't want to move out immediately.

5. There are "paper" changes you can do during the extended closing. For example you could change the zoning, draw up floor plans, get a plat approved, start the paperwork on a condo-conversion etc.

Students often ask me, "Why would you work on a property before you own it?" They also ask, "What if you do a bunch of work on it before closing and then the seller decides not to sell it to you?" These are great questions because, it would be terrible to spend a lot of money on a piece of property and then not end up owning it. Here are a few rules I use to handle this issue.

First, always make sure you have written permission from the seller to do the work. Second, always record the purchase contract as a lien against the title of the property. You will need the seller's permission to do this but by agreeing to let you do the work and agreeing to the contract there should be no problem. This is a great way to have some legal protection if the seller tries to back-out of the contract after the work is completed.

Third, do not do any physical work to a property if sellers are still occupying it. This may become a problem if they like what you are doing to the property and want to stay.

Fourth, do not pay your subcontractors in full until after the closing. That way you can ask them to put a lien on the property for their work if the seller doesn't close. If this happens the seller will own the property but it will have a bunch of liens on it. The subcontractors would now have the ability to foreclose on the property and since you will pay the contrator, you will have the lien. I have never had a deal come to this but it is further protection for the buyer.

Finally you can sue sellers for "specific performance". This means they agreed to the contract and they must perform. People must honor their contracts. They usually will if they face a court action that they know will most likely go in your favor. The way to avoid court, which is always my preference, is to take the precautionary steps I've outlined above.

An extended closing can lower your carrying costs significantly. By doing it carefully and covering your bases it can be a fantastic "seller financing" tool for your deals. Keep this technique in mind if it fits your deal. You might as well get as much done as possible while someone *else* is paying for the property!

7. Open-Ended Closing:

An "Open-Ended Closing" gives you the same benefits of the "Extended Closing" but for an open-ended period of time. In other words there is *no set date* for when you will close on the property. In this case a closing date is determined by *connecting the closing date plus earnest money and obligation to buy, to a milestone.*

Let's assume you are buying a lot where you can build 15 condominiums. When you make your offer you might put a clause, similar to one of these, in the terms of your offer: "Closing will be 7 days after the city approves a building permit"; "If the city does not approve a building permit all earnest monies will be refunded to the buyer. In addition the buyer will be released of all obligations to this contract"; "Closing will be 21 days after final plats are approved". If the property is a multi-family property you are buying for rental income the clause might say, "Closing will be within 48 hours of all units being occupied".

You can tie a closing date to *anything*. I've had a project with a student in Southern California which did not close for over a year because the closing was tied to something that ended up taking much longer than we originally thought. The city changed some rules and we had to get a variance to make the project work. Had we been paying interest on a loan during that time it would have hurt the deal tremendously. Because of the "Open-ended Closing" it did not matter at all. The seller paid the cost of holding the property during that time.

If you are doing a deal based on a change that is not guaranteed, _always_ use an "Open-ended Closing".

8. Seller partnerships:

A seller partnership means the seller stays involved with the deal _during the change of use._ The seller puts the property into the deal in exchange for part of the profits. As an example let's say you find a property with a much "Higher and Better" use. When you talk to the seller about purchasing the property the seller becomes very interested in your project. Here is what can happen if you create a partnership.

The seller can put the property in your name without charging you for the property until the changes are complete and the property is re-sold. At the time of the sale the seller will receive the money for the property _and_ the agreed-upon portion of the profits. If they pay for the _changes_ to the property you can increase their percentage of profits.

Essentially the property is now possibly the seller's contribution to the deal. The seller brings the property and the cost to change to the table and you bring expertise and leg work. This is a sensational option because you have no carrying costs on the property itself during purchase, changes or sale! Talk about saving a ton of money. This is the ultimate in seller financing.

I always offer the seller a partnership as an option. This is because if it is accepted you have the best of both worlds. (Profit with no financial investment) If it is refused, however, you can always say later it was offered. Wording for this might read, "Seller was offered a partnership with buyer for profit and refused in order to receive their profits at an earlier date." This has proved beneficial later when a seller was mad I had made a profit on the property. When I reminded him I had offered him a partnership he didn't have much left to say.

The final note on seller partnerships is this: In 15 years of doing these types of transactions I've never had a seller take me up on the offer to form a partnership. I'm not saying it wouldn't happen but typically sellers do not want to partner, they want to *sell* their property. The reality is most people are selling their property because of some certain need. Choosing to partner with buyers usually does not meet the need that caused them to sell in the first place. However, some sellers who are getting large cash proceeds from me at closing will often be willing to contribute some of that cash to the deal for a return. Check out the next seller financing technique!

9. Seller Finance Boomerang

I named this technique the "Seller Finance Boomerang" because essentially any cash you put into the deal boomerangs right back to you. In short this is a form of seller financing where the seller finances the *changes* to the property.

(Bear with me until the end of this section as this will not seem like seller financing at first.) To begin with you are going to actually pay cash, in some form or other for a piece of property. You will come up with your own cash, raise capital from investors or get a loan. Then, immediately after closing and funding of the profits to the seller, the seller will then *loan those profits back to you*. You will now pay the seller an interest rate in return for that cash.

Now you can use the cash the seller loans back to you to make changes to the property *and* pay the loan payments! Finally, the seller is repaid with interest when you re-sell the property. The seller is happy because of making interest on their investment during the time of the property improvements. Therefore, the seller ends up making even more on the deal than was initially conceived.

Another reason why a seller might be willing to do this concerns our economy. At this time in our economy (2009) the real estate market is quite slow in many locations. Lots of people are having a tough time selling. Sometimes any kind of sale is appealing. If they are leery about wrapping their mortgage or you carrying their equity then the "Seller Finance Boomerang" technique might appeal to them. It is a great way to show them you are able to raise capital and thereby increase their trust.

You may have some more questions such as, "Since you are using the *property itself* to raise capital wouldn't a "Seller Finance Boomerang" increase your carrying costs?" and "Wouldn't you even possibly now have *two* loans on one property?"

The answer to both of these questions is yes, but here is why you might want to do a "Seller Finance Boomerang" anyway. In my system "The Foundation to Success" I teach you to only buy properties which have a "Higher and Better" use. In most cases it costs money to take a property from where it is now to that "Higher and Better" use and this is one way for you to finance that shift. (It is probably the easiest and cheapest way.)

Sellers have the option to boomerang as much or as little as they wish back to you for changes. You might as well use the cash you raised, to *buy* the property *and* pay for the changes!

THE 10TH WAY TO SELLER FINANCE PROPERTIES

THE 10TH WAY TO SELLER FINANCE PROPERTIES

The final method of seller financing deserves a chapter of its own. This method is called "Buying LLC's" (Limited Liability Companies). This doesn't mean you are just going to go out and buy companies. It means when you find a property that fits your investment criteria that is already owned by a corporation, you might consider buying the corporation rather than just the property.

In this instance we are encompassing the meaning of seller financing to include the property coming with its own financing. (You don't have to go get a *new* loan.) Here is how it works. When you buy an LLC that owns a property, the property is included when you purchase the corporation.

One of the major benefits of buying a property this way is it allows you to avoid a traditional closing on the property and the associated fees. In addition the LLC will most likely come with financing in place for the property. (This is the seller financing part.)

One of the benefits of buying an LLC which owns property is the loan you are taking over may have been in service for several years. Imagine buying an LLC that originally had a 15-year mortgage on the piece of property included in it, but 5 years of payments have already been made on the loan. If this is the case then large portions of each payment will go to principal. We call this a serviced or seasoned mortgage. In addition it will be paid off in 10 years!

Let's look a little closer at the cost savings of buying a property in this manner. If an LLC sells a *building* it owns but remains the LLC then commissions, closing costs, capital gains taxes, recapture taxes, etc., would all have to be paid. In addition when a property is on the market the managers of the LLC will usually negotiate the price and, in todays market, may have to accept a lower than full price offer.

If instead the *LLC*, (which owns the property) is sold, the sale of the property would be included yet the majority of those fees would not apply. A savvy buyer would figure out the costs of those fees and then offer the LLC a purchase price for the LLC that includes whatever equity *remains* in the property, *minus* the above types of closing fees (or less). This would give you as the buyer an immediate and very handsome return on your investment while giving the sellers a fair amount of cash compared to just selling their property.

There are also some banking perks you get when you buy an LLC. If you own an LLC that has been around for some time it is considered to be "tenured". This means it has its own tax returns and history of property management and cash flow. When it is tenured it is much easier to get operating lines of credit than it is with a *new* LLC. In addition, refinancing the existing mortgage is easier since the LLC has owned the building for some time now, possibly many years.

Consider the following example:

"ACME LLC" owns a 10-unit apartment complex. It has been owned for 8 years. The LLC bought the property for $500,000 and now it's worth $700,000. $400,000 is still owed on the 15-year loan. This loan has only 7 remaining years of payments. If you stop here it seems like there is $300,000 of equity in the property. (Or LLC) But let's take a look at what else is part of the picture.

The following numbers show what a sale of this property separate from the LLC might look like. We will assume that during the time of ownership roughly $160,000 was depreciated.

(I've rounded the numbers to the thousand for simplicity)

Asking Price	$700,000
Less Discount of 5%- (Buyer decides not to pay full price.)	-$35,000
Less Commissions of 5% on $665,000	-$33,000
Less Closing Costs of 2% of $665,000	-$13,000
Less amount to pay off of existing loan	-$400,000
Equals (Net cash to seller before tax issues)	**$219,000**
Less Capital Gains Tax on a gain of *$119,000* ($219,000 minus the original $100,000 down payment, times 15% long-term gain tax rate.)	-$18,000
Less Recapture Tax on $160,000 (Depreciated amount) at up to 25%	-$40,000
Net to Seller after all costs (Or, actual equity!)	**$161,000**

As you can see, the assumed $300,000 of equity is misleading and in reality may be much less. In this case by showing the seller the above type of chart, your offer to buy the LLC for $161,000 or even less might make good sense. The majority of the true profits will still be captured by the seller, yet some of the hassle of selling the property will be avoided.

Imagine if you could buy an LLC, that owns a financed property with $300,000 in equity and a mortgage that only has 8 years left on it, for $161,000 or less! In this example you would be paying roughly 50 cents on the dollar for the equity. What a deal for the seller and the buyer!

There are quite a few details you should consider and then discuss with an attorney and tax expert before buying an LLC. First of all, just because you helped the seller avoid capital gains and recapture tax doesn't mean you won't have to pay them. Second, you will be responsible for anything the corporation owes to any creditors. Third, you will need to make sure the LLC does not have any other outstanding liabilities. Meaning there are no prior bad acts that could come back to haunt you and the LLC is in good standing in the community. Your attorneys can inform you of other things to consider if you decide to attempt this technique.

There are only two ways in which I would personally buy an LLC containing property as described above. The reason I am careful with this purchase and sale is because, if I wanted to sell this property and *take out* my cash profits, I would then have to pay the capital gains and recapture taxes the first seller avoided.

The first way I would be willing to buy this property is if I make sure to only sell the LLC in the same way I purchased it. That means I would sell the LLC to someone else, not the property on its own. The other way is to sell the property *within a 1031 exchange*. This is a tax deferral program where you buy another property with the proceeds from the sale of the first property and never touch those proceeds. Talk with your CPA and tax attorney to get all of the details on this technique.

These 10 techniques discussed in the last 2 chapters cover the majority of the different types of seller financing I teach and have used. Once you understand them and are able to use them in your own transactions you will be able to unleash your true investing power! Read through them again and if at the end of this book you still have questions consider attending an "Advanced Seller Financing" Degree Camp.

FREE Online Resources

Another option for you is to visit my website at **www.mikewatsoninvesting.com** and go to "The MWI Community Forum". There you can search for answers to questions or even post your personal questions. Students, staff, coaches and I will answer your questions there free of charge.

My intent is for you to be able to not only learn this material but use it. In order to use it you must have a clear understanding of the material and therefore must be able to have your questions answered.

In the next chapter I will explain how most seller financing transactions are written up. Also see Chapter 19 titled "Do Not Forget These!" for some bonus items to remember when using seller financing for investment deals.

CHAPTER **8**

HOW DOES THE PAPERWORK WORK?

HOW DOES THE
PAPERWORK WORK?

know when you see the word paperwork you might be ready to nod off. I'll do my best to make it quick. My advice is to talk with a reputable title company in your area. Make an appointment with a closing agent who has been in the business for many years. This person will be quite familiar with the different types of paperwork required for buying and selling real estate using seller financing.

The two main things you need to understand are the "Note" and the "Deed of Trust". The "Note" is the paperwork that creates a loan. A "*Promissory* Note" in most cases does not involve collateral. Meaning that it is basically an "I owe you" with no named asset backing its worth. A promissory note is based on a promise to pay the loan back.

Typically a "Note" (without the promissory part) will be *attached* to something and this "something" is then considered collateral. (In our case it is real estate.) This collateral is what is at "risk" if the person to whom the note is extended does not make payments on time or pay the note back in full when it is due.

The method of *attaching* the note to something when that something is real estate is called a "Deed of Trust". You could call the deed of trust the glue that sticks the note to the real estate.

In traditional purchases you buy a property and get a loan on it. This means a bank or mortgage company will extend a loan to you using paperwork called a "Note" and then will attach that note to the property using the "Deed of Trust" with the right to take the property back (foreclose) if you do not follow the exact terms of the "Note". The same thing happens with seller financing. The difference is the seller is the person who can take your property back rather than the bank or mortgage company.

Another type of paperwork is used when you "wrap" a loan. In that case a title company will typically use what is called an "All-Inclusive Trust Deed and Note" (AITD). This means the original loan that remains on the property is included as part of the collateral. As we discussed before, the AITD means the seller's note blankets or wraps the original loan the seller had on the property.

Once we get into some of the subtleties of seller financing we will talk about other types of paperwork or clauses you will want to incorporate into your offers. I always recommend using a professional when writing contracts if it is not an area with which you are familiar. Contracts are binding and can't be changed once they are agreed upon and signed by both parties. So, when making offers always ensure your contract matches your *intent*. Let professionals help you achieve this goal. Now let's move on to some more details of seller financing.

CHAPTER **9**

YOU CAN CREATE ANYTHING
WITH SELLER FINANCING

CHAPTER **9**

YOU CAN CREATE ANYTHING WITH SELLER FINANCING

One type of seller financing we discussed is called free and clear seller financing. Remember this means the seller has no loans on the property and is willing to provide some or all of the financing. As I mentioned before, this is my favorite type of seller financing due to its flexibility. The only two people who need to be satisfied are the buyer and the seller. This means you can create any terms you want!

I have an incredible example of this type of financing used by one of my students. This student, Sandy, solved some serious issues with a property at the last minute and saved the deal using seller financing. Let me show you how.

Sandy found a lot in her area of expertise with a small home on it that needed some repairs. The property was a corner lot and was quite large. Because she knew the development standards and zoning, she knew the city would allow her to build a second unit on the property to create a duplex. After she had the duplex built she could do a condo-conversion and sell the properties as two separate condos. If this deal went as planned there was about $150,000 of profit or increase in equity that would occur.

Sandy contacted the owner by letter. (Along with everyone else in the area because it was her "Area of Expertise" as explained fully in "The Foundation to Success" taught in my book, "The Highest and Best Real Estate Investment".) The owner telephoned about a week later and said the property was already under contract to someone else. However, she would call Sandy if it fell through.

My student convinced the seller to take a back-up offer just in case. The seller didn't want to consider seller financing because she already had a contract without it. Sandy was a little disappointed because she had discovered the owner did not have a loan on the property. She knew it would be in the seller's best interest to do the seller financing.

Regardless, it was such a good deal she decided she would still be able to raise capital to make the deal work. Well, it just so happened only two days later she got a call from the seller. The other deal had fallen apart and she wanted to take the student's back-up offer.

Here is how the deal looked. Sandy would be paying $200,000 for the property. She talked with her power team and 3 members wanted to be partners on the deal by putting in some of their own funds. Each partner put in $20,000. With these funds as a down payment she was able to get a bank loan on the property to include the cost of building the second unit.

She got her loan approved, collected the funds from the 3 investors and was set to close the deal. Two days before closing Sandy found out that even though the property was *zoned* for the second unit, there were very old subdivision deed restrictions that did *not* allow for a second unit on the property. This was horrible news. It meant the bank would not do the loan and she would not be able to buy the property. She called the seller to give them the bad news.

The seller already had a new home under contract and was supposed to close on it that week. Talk about a real estate nightmare! The seller asked Sandy to reconsider or figure out a way the property could still be purchased. So, Sandy's power team went to work. (Learn how to set up your own power team in my first book, "The Highest and Best Real Estate Investment!")

One of the members of the team had some experience with title work. She discovered a state law showing a way to allow a person to change a deed restriction. The only thing was it would take at least 3-6 months to get the change made. This was too long for the seller to wait.

So, here is what Sandy proposed to the seller. She asked the seller to sell her the property with very short term seller financing. $60,000 was offered as a down payment from the funds she had raised from her team. That was enough money for the seller to buy the new home.

Then Sandy told the seller there was only one issue left to worry about. This issue involved getting the deed restrictions changed so the second unit could be built. Without this, the property was not nearly as valuable. With two units the property would eventually potentially be worth over $600,000 but with only one unit it would only be worth $300,000 after fully re-building a new home. Thus the profits were much less. (Or even non-existent) To compensate for this risk Sandy asked the seller if the *loan amount could fluctuate* depending on whether or not the restrictions were changed.

What this meant was Sandy would buy the property so the seller could buy a new home and then Sandy would do everything in her power to change the deed restrictions. If she got them changed the loan would remain the same. If she didn't, part of the seller financed loan would be forgiven. The seller agreed.

Sandy set to work doing all the necessary things to change the deed restrictions. At the same time she had the property for sale. (See the Flixer section in my first book)

Sandy ended up selling the property to a developer within a couple of months; unfortunately it was prior to the deed restrictions being able to be changed. (The property would have been worth *much* more if they had been changed.) The seller lowered the loan amount just a small amount at that next closing. The next buyer after Sandy was the one who ended up changing the restrictions and developing the property.

Seller financing saved this deal and made it work for everyone including Sandy, her Power Team and the seller. The seller was paid in time to purchase the new home. The buyer and her power team still made a small profit.

This is an extremely important example of how seller financing can make or break a deal. It is also a fantastic demonstration of how *flexible* it can be and how important it is to know the needs and the situation of the seller. My guess is that if this had been a typical investor rather than one of my students who had learned to expand her thinking, this deal would have fallen through. The seller would not have been able to close on a new home and it would have been a disaster.

The most interesting terms of this transaction were in the flexibility of the loan *after* closing or the *payoff amount of the loan*. What made this deal work was the option for the seller to adjust the loan amount for the buyer if the buyer was unable to attain the change of deed restriction. If this hadn't been an option the buyer would not have been able to go through with the deal. The risk would have been too high. In traditional financing you would be hard pressed to find a bank or mortgage company that would agree to terms like those!

Let's move on and take a look at one of the most incredible terms you can negotiate with seller financing.

CHAPTER 10
"GREEN" MORTGAGES

CHAPTER **10**

"GREEN" MORTGAGES

The time has come to talk about this concept of a "green" mortgage. First I'll talk about just what is a "green" mortgage. Next I'll give you a little background and then some insight into how to get or create a "green" mortgage.

A "green" mortgage is a mortgage that can be used over and over again. Just like recyclable materials it can move from one buyer to another and another. Essentially a "green" mortgage is a mortgage containing a clause which states the loan is assumable. It could be assumable with some qualifying or it could be a completely non-qualifying loan. If it is non-qualifying then *anyone* (who can legally buy a property) can assume the loan. This is the ultimate "green" mortgage.

Let me give you a little background about assumable loans. Assumable loans have been around for years. Many types of bank loans are assumable as are lots of commercial loans. As a matter of fact even government loans (FHA) used to be assumable by people who did *not* have to qualify.

When the savings and loan industry went under in the late 1980's many lenders did not want to give assumable loans anymore. They felt these types of loans were more risky once they were assumed because the person who was now making the payment did not have to qualify for the loan. This may be true in some instances but what if the value of the property has gone up? Isn't the bank still able to foreclose? Wouldn't they still get the asset back? Even though this is not an ideal situation it is something for a bank to consider when evaluating the risk of an assumption.

Something else to consider about this supposed risk is the true effect of having an assumable loan on a property. What effect does it have? Quite simply it makes the property *more valuable*. Let me show you why. If, for instance, there is a home for sale that does *not* have a "green" mortgage on it, you as the buyer must go to a bank, go through the entire lending process, qualify for a loan, pay loan fees and then buy the home. Not everyone can do that.

Because of this fact alone the market for buyers is diminished. *When you have a market with fewer buyers you will get a lower price for your product.* This is a fact from basic economics. It is the relationship between supply and demand. The same thing happens in the fuel market. When the demand for gasoline is high and the supply is low then the prices go up. If the demand was low and there was a glut of gasoline then prices would go down. This is how open markets work. There is a bit more to it but this is essentially how real estate works as well. Therefore, if you can get a "green" mortgage on a piece of property you will have automatically increased its value by the mere fact of there being more available buyers.

Just what does it take to create a "green" mortgage? One of the ways you can create an assumable mortgage is to get the current lender to remove the "Due on Sale" clause. We will talk about this option at length during the "How to find sellers who are RIPE for giving you seller financing" Chapter. When a lender removes the "Due on Sale" clause they are making that loan "wrappable" and even assumable if they add an assumption clause. In a market where there are lots of foreclosures (as we are experiencing in 2009) this is a reasonable request you can make of a lender.

Another way to create a "green" mortgage is to ask sellers to let their seller financed loan be assumable when you sell the property. If the sellers agree you can either omit the "Due on Sale Clause" that is typically written into a note, or you can put in a simple assumption clause allowing the loan to be assumed. One of the biggest benefits for the seller is this lowers the chance of the loan being paid off. You might think this is a negative but sellers think passive income from the seller financed note is a *great* thing. Why would sellers want this to stop? If the loan is assumable they will most likely keep getting interest payments for a longer period of time.

Sellers may be slow to agree to this at first. They may not trust another person as much as they have come to trust you. If you come across this situation you might explain to the seller that the next buyer will have a much larger vested interest in the deal than you do. Tell them you are going to require the next buyer to put a down payment into the purchase. This will reduce the likelihood of a default on the loan.

Some other options to help the seller be willing to allow an assumption might be for you to have the seller put language in the loan that makes the interest payment *increase* whenever the loan is assumed. If you do this the payments will get higher and higher each time someone assumes the loan. You also might include a fee (possibly a percent of the loan) that goes to the seller each time the loan is assumed.

Using these ideas the seller may end up with a person paying on their loan who has more money invested in the deal, plus the seller may periodically receive a lump sum of money, and/or higher income. These options can often be quite attractive to a seller.

There are many ways to help sellers overcome their worry of the loan being assumable. Keep reading as this is a major topic. I am going to give you tool after tool to create "green" mortgages.

Now that you understand the history and concept of a "green" mortgage, and have an idea of how to get a seller to let you create a "green" mortgage, let me explain how one will help in today's real estate market.

In 2009 there are several problems with mortgages. Banks and mortgage companies have become extremely tight with their money. There is less, and in some cases *no* money to lend and therefore qualifying standards have been made much more stringent than in the previous 5-10 years.

As a result there has been a dampening of real estate sales. Buyers with less than perfect credit and income do not have *anywhere* to go to get loans. They must wait until the loan market loosens up again in order to buy. This lowering of demand makes the prices drop. When the prices drop, buyers will also wait until they think the market will pick up again. They don't want to buy when the prices are going down. This compounds the effect of fewer buyers in the market.

There is interesting fallout from all of these factors. What has happened is there are many people who would like to buy a home but who cannot get a loan for one reason or another. This creates a "pent up" demand for housing. This is especially true for first-time home buyers.

When these buyers are empowered to buy, prices will stabilize and eventually start to go up again. However, the only way this will happen is to find a way for them to get a loan for property. Are you beginning to see the importance of a "green" mortgage?

This is the key! With assumable loans, people can buy and sellers can tap into that pent up demand and sell their home faster than other homes on the market.

When you create mortgages and then make those mortgages assumable, or "green", then you will have helped with the credit crunch we are now experiencing.

"Green" mortgages, or assumable mortgages are powerful enough to improve the real estate market.

~Mike Watson

THE 23 MOST POWERFUL TERMS TO NEGOTIATE WITH SELLER FINANCING

THE 23 MOST POWERFUL TERMS TO NEGOTIATE WITH SELLER FINANCING

Most people think of "terms" as the price and the timing of a transaction. Terms are much more than just those two items. Well thought out terms can make it easy for you to buy properties. Terms can create a huge cash flow during ownership and can even make your deal sell faster in the future.

The first thing you must understand is *you* have complete control over any of your deals. What I mean is *you* make the decision to buy or not. Therefore you are in control. With this control comes incredible power when you are negotiating. But what specific terms should you negotiate?

Traditionally negotiated terms include price, date of closing, length of option period, amount seller will pay for repairs, which title company to use, etc. When you are looking at a deal it is wise to ask the other party about all the different options for terms before you even go to the negotiating table. But first you must know the benefit of those terms and how you can use them to negotiate with sellers in order to make the deal work better for both of you.

When you are getting ready to write offers, *give the sellers what they want* and then build the rest of the terms to make the deal attractive for *you*. Typically the seller's main concern is the price. Keep in mind, there are ways to make a full price (or even higher) offer work if the seller is willing to do seller financing.

Here are a few of the terms you can negotiate. On all of these items I will assume the seller is agreeing to seller finance. Use this list as a starting point to allow your mind to expand into a new territory of negotiations. I will give you a quick synopsis of the list so you can refer back to the terms easily. Then I will explain each term in detail as some will most likely be new ideas.

Ask the sellers if they will do the following... (The Terms)

1. Take a lower interest rate on their seller financing.
2. Give you an adjustable rate on their seller financing. (Up or down whichever suits your deal best.)
3. Allow you to make *interest only* payments.
4. Allow you to have no interest and make principal-only payments.
5. Allow you to make quarterly or yearly payments rather than monthly.
6. Let you make no payments until the whole loan is due.
7. Let you amortize the loan over a long period. (Like 50 years)
8. Let you have your down payment back to use on changes to this property or other deals.
9. Put on a pre-payment penalty. (This means you don't have to pay it off!)
10. Lower the payoff amount based on circumstances.
11. Allow you to defer payments on one or more of the loans.
12. Allow financing to be assumed by someone who does *not* have to qualify.
13. Allow the loan to be assumed by someone who *does* have to qualify.
14. Allow their loan to be assumed if they get paid a fee and/or a higher rate when it is assumed.

15. Allow the loan to be split up, (splintered) and assumed.
16. Sign a subordination agreement allowing a different person or entity to be the first lien.
17. Extend the closing date.
18. Allow you to do changes prior to closing.
19. Allow for a small or no down payment.
20. Pay for some of the cost to make changes to the property.
21. Pay for closing costs.
22. Allow you to *re*-collateralize the loan. (also called cross-collateralize)
23. Allow you to *de*-collateralize the loan.

Hopefully by reading and understanding this list you will come up with even more ideas of your own to fit your deals. Here is a more detailed explanation of each of these terms and how you might use them.

1. Will the seller take a lower interest rate on their seller financing?

Even a small reduction in the interest rate can mean thousands of dollars of savings on a deal. Always negotiate for as low an interest rate as possible unless there are other more important terms, such as getting a seller to actually offer seller financing in the first place.

A fun thing you can try to do is to re-negotiate the interest rate right before closing. I've had some success with this technique in the past. What you do is ask them flat out if they will exchange a lower interest rate for a higher price or some kind of bonus. I've offered a boat (to a boat lover) and even a motorcycle to a seller to get them to lower the interest rate. In both cases it worked!

Get that interest rate lowered for as an extended period as possible. (Make sure to calculate your savings so you don't offer them more than your savings.) In one example, I got a 2% reduction on a $200,000 loan for 5 years which amounted to $20,000 when I offered the seller an $8,000 dollar boat. He was excited to get a boat. I was excited to get a lower interest rate!

2. Will the seller give you an adjustable rate on their seller financing? (Up or down whichever suits your deal best.)

This can be a fantastic tool to use if you plan to own the property for a short time. You can ask the seller to take a lower rate at the beginning of the term and then increase the rate. In this case it makes no difference to you when the rate goes up because you will be selling it. If there is a chance you will keep the property in your long term portfolio make sure you can refinance or that the interest payments do not go so high as to become a financial burden.

The other time you could use this technique is when you buy an income producing property. Let's say you are buying an apartment complex and the seller is asking $1,000,000 for the property. Through determining market rents and occupancy rates you realize the property is only about 70% rented and at *low* rates. The market shows occupancy rates are more like 90% in the area. The problem is the seller's asking price reflects the property being rented at *market* rents and 95% occupancy.

In this situation you could offer to give the seller the full price but you could tie the interest rate on the seller finance note to the occupancy rate. In other words you could pay 3% on the loan until the property hit 75% occupancy, then 4% until it hit 80% occupancy and so on. You must make sure to have a cap on both ends. It should not ever go up too high or down too low. Make it fit the property and the market.

When you do this you are essentially having the seller set the property's debt service equal to the true value. If the seller insists it is worth as much as their asking price and will be able to be rented at the higher occupancy rate then the terms should be agreeable.

If the seller won't do this you should ask for an extended or open-ended closing tied to the occupancy rate. Then you can wait to close until the occupancy is where it should be based on the market. When you make this suggestion you may find the seller might like the adjustable rate idea much better as it will not hold up the closing.

3. Will the seller allow you to make *interest-only* payments?

What this means is instead of paying down the principal part of the loan on each payment, for a set period of time you only pay interest. This can be a way to have your property produce positive cash flow from day one.

During negotiations, be sure to remember to mention the following benefit to your seller: "No capital gains taxes will have to be paid until some or all of the principle of the loan is received by the seller." This can be a big benefit and may help in negotiations. (Check with a CPA)

The interesting thing about this is the seller still gets income without lowering the balance owed. Be sure and point out the seller will get payments over time and then when it comes time for the loan to be paid off the entire amount of the original loan will still be owed! The majority of seller financing notes I set up with sellers have interest-only payments.

4. Will the seller allow you to have no interest and make principal payments only?

Sometimes sellers only care about getting their asking price. They feel they *must* get their price. This is a great time to tell them, "OK, I'll give you your price." Then tell them you will pay them in monthly installments of a percentage of the total price for a fixed time.

You can save tons of money on a deal this way. This is a zero interest rate! You can even pay them *more* than their asking price and still do well with this technique. Your interest payments over time can add up to enormous amounts. If you can eliminate that part of the expense you can create some incredible deals for yourself.

5. Will the seller allow you to make quarterly or yearly payments rather than monthly?

I've already shown you an example where this was an ideal setup for the seller. A seller was going to sail up the Mississippi River and then possibly around the world for several years and didn't want to have to keep up with monthly payments. He was paid once a year so he only had to occasionally check his account. The great thing about this setup is you can raise capital or *accrue* rents for your yearly payments. This gives you more options than a monthly payment to the seller.

6. Will the seller let you pay all of the interest when the loan is due? (At the call or balloon time)

This means at the time you sell or refinance the property you will pay the seller the principal amount of the loan *plus* all of the interest that has accrued. It also means you don't have any payments the whole time you have the loan. Remember if you do this be sure and enter the *accruing* interest on your books so you know how much real debt is on the property when you go to refinance or sell it. Talk with your CPA on how this will affect your taxes.

Some sellers are quite happy to do this for you because it means they get more money at the end and have no worries about your payments.

Many sellers have income from other parts of their lives that supports their lifestyle without having to get payments on a loan made to you. The best case scenario would be they carry the loan for you and don't make you pay payments or accrue interest. Of course you would have to be a star negotiator to get that done!

7. Will the seller let you amortize the loan over a longer than "normal" period? (Such as 40-50 years)

This will make your payment lower because you won't be paying as much principal on each payment. Some sellers may want you to do this so they lock in an income for a long period of time. Once sellers get addicted to passive income with no property management some never want it to end.

8. Will the seller let you have your down payment back to use on changes to this property or other deals?

This is the "Seller Finance Boomerang" we talked about in the "9 Types of Seller Financing" section. It is always a fantastic question to ask your seller when you are negotiating. You might as well raise capital for your *project* from the seller.

9. Does the seller want you to put on a pre-payment penalty? (Secretly this means you don't have to pay it off!)

A pre-payment penalty is usually viewed negatively. It is an extra fee you have to pay to sellers if you pay off a loan before its due date.

People usually put these into loans to guarantee they get payments for a certain amount of time. They like getting interest and they want to keep making that income. They don't want their principal back!

To use this technique, ask if the sellers are interested in guaranteeing their payments. If they are, then offer to give them a pre-payment penalty. This way you guarantee the use of their loan for a long time! Now turn around and ask them for some things in return.

There are three things you want to remember when you agree to a loan with a pre-payment penalty. The first is the loan must be a "simple assumption". The reason for this is you can't be stuck with the property long term without *any* options. It allows you to sell the property to someone else who will assume the pre-payment penalty along with all of the other terms of the loan.

Second, there must be a subordination clause. This means you can get a construction loan on the property and the seller will subordinate (be the 2nd lien) to that loan without you incurring a penalty. If the seller doesn't agree to subordinate then it will be extremely difficult for you to get another loan on the property if it is needed for fix-up, construction down payment or any other reason.

Finally, they must agree to a re-collateralization clause. What this does is allow you to *move* the loan to a different piece of property so *it* can be the collateral for the loan. You will guarantee the seller will have as much or more equity behind the loan in the new property as they had in the first property.

These clauses allow you to have a pre-payment penalty while keeping your options open. In the mean time you increase the chance the sellers get those payments until the end of the pre-payment penalty which is what they really wanted in the first place. (I will talk more about these three items in later sections)

10. Will the seller lower the payoff amount based on circumstances?

What this means is the seller will start out with a loan amount of one amount, let's say $500,000 but when it comes time for the loan to be paid off, for whatever reason, the $500,000 could be lowered by a pre-determined amount based on circumstances.

A perfect example of this is the example I discussed previously where one of my students negotiated a lower payoff of the loan to accommodate the issue the property had with its deed restrictions.

There are many reasons you might need or want to negotiate a different payoff from the original loan amount. These include but are not limited to, the occupancy rate, the economy, the value of a property, and whether or not a higher and better use is agreed to by the city or county. This technique can make or break a deal by lowering the risk for the buyer and allowing a deal to consummate rather than fail.

11. Will the seller allow you to defer payments on one or more of the loans?

I love this technique because it can make an OK deal *outstanding*. Here is an example of how I used this idea to both my and the seller's benefit. I found a man and wife who owned an 8-plex they wanted to sell. This property had been causing contention in the couple's marriage and they wanted to sell it immediately.

The property was worth about $375,000 and they owed $275,000 on it which meant they had $100,000 in equity. They told me they would do whatever was necessary in order to get rid of the property. I ended up assuming their first loan of $275,000 which only had 8 years of payments remaining then had the sellers carry a second loan for $100,000.

I asked them before writing the offer if they wanted their cash or equity at the closing or if they wanted to turn it into income. They explained they had bought the property originally to have a retirement income. I asked them how soon they were planning on retiring and they told me in about 5 years.

At this point I suggested they give me a seller financed second for the $100,000 and I offered to *start payments on it in 5 years when they retired*. This way they would have all of their payments ahead of them and I could quickly buy the property from them. This solved their problems and I didn't have to raise a down payment.

We closed, their hassle disappeared and they no longer needed to do any property management. Finally, they now had retirement income in the form of those payments that would start in 5 years. They were ecstatic about this deal.

In addition, I really liked not having to make payments for 5 years on the second lien. I was able to use all of the net rents during those five years to make larger payments on the first mortgage than was required. By doing this I paid off the first lien in 4.5 years instead of the 8 years that remained on the mortgage. By the time the second lien payment had *started* the first lien was *paid for* and the rents had gone up considerably. This property became a fantastic cash flowing investment!

12. Will the seller allow the seller financing to be assumed by someone who does *not* have to qualify?

This means anyone can take over the loan when the proprty is sold. This is the most desirable type of loan for you as the buyer because it means the property is easy to sell and is worth more. There are more buyers that can buy, therefore the demand is higher. Higher demand, higher price, it is that simple.

Ideally a seller will allow you to let the loan be assumed by *anyone*. Use all of the tools in your box to help you achieve this golden opportunity. You can offer a higher interest rate, a longer term, a pre-payment penalty or even a higher down payment. If you get the seller to agree to the loan being assumed by any buyer then you have increased the value of the property, sometimes greatly. Here are some additional things you might offer to the seller as incentives:

A. Give the seller an increase in the interest rate when the loan is assumed. For instance, say you are able to negotiate 6% seller financing. You can put language into the loan saying the rate will increase by 1% each time it is assumed by a new buyer. This would give the seller a higher interest rate and therefore a higher monthly payment whenever the loan is assumed. This could be a huge motivator to get the seller to agree to give you an assumable loan.

B. Put an origination fee on the loan each time it is assumed. This is a fee the new buyer would pay to the old seller. Origination fees are used *regularly* when a buyer goes to a bank. The fees, usually a percent or two of the amount of the loan, are paid to the lender just for doing the loan.

    Offer the seller this little treat whenever someone assumes the loan. If it is a $200,000 loan whenever someone assumes it the seller might get $2,000. This is paid by the new buyer and is not an expense for you. What a great way to sweeten the pot for the seller at the time of the assumption.

C. Make the loan re-amortize to 30 years upon assumption. In other words, the loan starts over at the first month payment on a 30 year loan each time there is a new person who assumes the loan. This only works on a loan where principal and interest are both being paid.

    Imagine this scenario. Seven years ago you got a principal and interest loan from a seller and have been faithfully making all your payments. Now only 23 years of payments are remaining for the seller. If you sell the property at this point you can make the new buyer's clock start ticking at the beginning of 30 years. The loan balance would stay the same but the amount of *time* the first seller would continue to get payments would lengthen as would the amount of interest they would eventually receive!

This allows the seller to get 37 years of payments instead of 30. You might think a seller would then be receiving a lower payment if the 23 year balance is re-amortized, but you can re-amortize at a higher rate than was in the original the loan. This could give the seller extra years and an equal to, or higher payment than they were receiving for the first 7 years of the original 30 year term.

D.   You could re-set the interest term on an interest only loan. This could be *very* exciting for sellers for several reasons. First it allows sellers to delay capital gains taxes because they don't receive their principal. This also makes your debt service lower. If you set up a loan for 10 years with interest only payments and then pay on it for 4 years, obviously, there are only 6 years remaining.

At the time of an assumption by a new buyer you could re-set the loan to revert back to ten years of interest payments. In essence the clock starts over again. Sellers are usually extremely excited about this because interest is all gravy. They can keep income coming in for a long time if it gets assumed over and over. Plus their principal is never touched!

These are just some of the incredible ways you can entice sellers to allow the loans to be assumed by someone who technically doesn't qualify. If your sellers still won't agree, always make a serious effort to at least have the loan be assumable by a "qualified" buyer. This way you are keeping the mortgage alive (GREEN) instead of killing it and having to start a new mortgage with a bank.

13. Will the seller allow the loan to be assumed by someone who *does* have to qualify?

Regardless of any other negotiating you should always ask the seller to let the loan be assumable. I would even go as far as to say this may be the most important term you want to get from the seller when you get seller financing! An assumable loan is more attractive to the next buyer because there are less costs and headache to assume a loan than there are to get a new loan. This is especially true in today's economy where loans are getting harder to obtain even by very qualified borrowers. This makes the property worth *much* more to you.

Sellers are often hesitant to let the loan be assumable, but one way to ease their minds is to allow *them* to help you set the qualifying standards for any buyer you might sell the property to in the future. Here are some things that can be used as qualifying standards. All of which are still much easier on a borrower than getting a full bank loan:

A. A minimum score of 600 on their credit report. This number sounds low, but it is actually the low end benchmark for FHA and VA loans.

B. A specific amount of down payment. This is a great qualifying standard. It is unique because *you* might get a 100% seller financing loan but then you might require at least a 5-10% down from the *new* buyer. You will have raised your sales price so the down payment will go to you, not the original seller. This benefits the original seller because the new buyer has a down payment that can be lost if loan payments are not made. They have a vested interest even though it is not directly with the old owner.

C. Another thing you can do is require anyone who assumes the
loan to have a cosigner. This gives the seller another reason
to believe in the replacement buyer and makes assumptions
easier.

What if after all your discussion about non-qualifying and qualifying assumptions and all of the incentives you offer, the seller is still
worried? The next term is our last ditch effort to keep a mortgage
"Green".

14. Will the seller allow their loan to be assumed just *one* time?

Often sellers just don't want their loan to be assumable. They may
be thinking, "I'm OK giving *you* a loan but I don't know anything
about the next person who might assume the loan." This is a valid
point. Sometimes you can get a seller to entertain the idea of an assumable loan with the items we talked about above. Others are still
hesitant. When you have very hesitant sellers the last thing you have
in your back pocket is to ask them to make the loan assumable just *one
time*. Consider the following example.

My second investment career deal was the purchase of a little condominium that was previously part of a hotel complex. It had been
converted to a condo project years before. An agent in my first real
estate office knew I was interested in being an investor and he told
me he had a listing of three condos in this project and the seller would
consider seller financing.

The units were each 2 bedroom and 1 bath and were about 800
square feet in size. All three were rented for $450 each per month. The
asking price in 1994 was $34,900 for each unit. The gentleman selling
the property wanted $5,000 down per unit and would carry a note for
the balance at 8% interest over a 30-year term. I didn't have a lot of
money so $5,000 down for each of the three units was a big commit-

ment even though the numbers looked good. I didn't have the courage in those early days to really negotiate the issue of the down payment. Now, of course, I wish I had bought all three units.

The price was good, but the property did present some problems. The purchase price wasn't high enough for regular banks and mortgage companies to offer decent financing for the project. They wanted a ton of money down or a very high interest rate or both. I thought if I ever wanted to sell, I would also have to seller finance. To address this issue I asked the seller if he would make it an assumable loan. He said, "No."

If you stop and think about it, a simple assumption mortgage can be quite daunting. The thought that for years and years after the sale of your property, anyone could pick up your mortgage without any input from you might make you very nervous too. I ended up telling the seller I would buy his unit only if *I* could sell it as well. He was having problems selling because of the financing and later, I would too. My compromise was I would purchase the unit if he allowed the loan to be a simple assumption only *one time.*

We put language in the contract that would allow me to sell once with a simple assumption and then the mortgage would no longer be assumable. He agreed and I closed on the property. I held it 19 months and sold it for a $20,000 profit. I sold the property for around $55,000. The new buyer had a $20,000 down payment and assumed my loan.

I look back at that now, and think how the terms of the deal were way ahead of my experience and understanding. Very few people complete seller financing deals, much less include assumable seller financing with a one-time clause in it.

This is a fantastic tool for today's market. Sellers will agree to many things now they would not normally because of the slower market. Don't be afraid to negotiate for what you want. The seller I worked with didn't really want to agree to these terms, but had no other choice. There are enough good deals out there right now that you can take time to find people who will work with you to get the very best terms to make a winning situation for both of you. Don't waste your time with people who won't.

 Do absolutely everything possible to keep a mortgage "Green"!

~**Mike Watson**

15. Will the seller allow the loan to be split up, (splintered) and assumed?

When you buy a property and you intend to increase the number of owners by building more units, subdividing the lot, or doing a condo conversion, you must get the seller to agree to split up the loan. That way when you sell the individual units the new buyer can have clear title to the property.

(I will discuss this in more detail in a later chapter when I talk about splintering.)

16. Will the seller sign a subordination agreement allowing a different person or entity to be the first lien? (Necessary if you are getting a first lien on the property through a bank.)

When you get a first lien on a property and the sellers are going to give you a second lien for their part of the financing, you must have an agreement that subordinates the 2nd lien to the first lien. The seller must agree to be the 2nd lien. They are giving up 1st lien rights. These rights are to be paid first in a foreclosure. If the sellers do not agree to subordinate to a first lien holder, a bank will usually not give you a loan at all. (I will talk much more about this issue in a later section.)

17. Will the seller extend the closing date?

Again, by extending the closing date you are getting the seller to carry the cost of the property for a longer period of time. This works well when you are planning on making changes to the property that will enhance its value *prior* to closing. It is also nice to have a little extra time to raise some additional capital.

18. Will the seller allow you to do changes prior to closing?

When there are changes that *can* be done prior to closing, it is in your best interest to *do* them prior to closing. Sometimes those changes require written permission from the seller. When you want to take a property through steps at the city to get a site plan or building permit, you will usually need the seller's permission or you will need to own the property.

19. Will the seller allow for a small or no down payment?

If the deal is a great deal and will cash flow without a down payment, then why make one? Negotiate as low a down payment as the seller will allow. Find out what the seller's needs are and see if you can meet those needs. Remind sellers that the lower the down payment, the higher the income they will receive over time!

20. Will the seller pay for some of the costs to make changes?

A seller could pay for fencing, upgrades, permits, landscaping, etc.

This is a fantastic tool when you are *required* to do upgrades.

On a deal I did a few years ago, the seller wanted a certain price. I agreed to the price but told him the price that he was asking was for an "improved" lot with curbs, gutters, fencing, etc. He agreed to pay for these things without raising the asking price.

This was an incredible opportunity for me because as this property was being developed the city would tell me such things as; I *"had"* to put up a cement wall costing me much more than the planned vinyl fence. The seller always attended these meetings and helped fight for the lower cost product. The city almost always agreed because it wasn't the "evil developer" who was asking for the changes. By having the seller be financially responsible for the required changes I was able to keep the costs of the deal low enough to provide a fantastic profit!

21. Will the seller pay for closing costs?

If you give sellers a good price it is not unreasonable to ask them to pay for a portion or even all of the closing costs. They can pay for any commissions, title fees, etc. that are a part of the deal. I have had sellers come to closing with more cash than I did because they had agreed to pay some of the closing costs. When you are doing seller financing there is no lender sitting in the background telling you who can pay for what. So, why not ask?

22. Will the seller allow you to *re*-collateralize the loan?

Re-collateralization occurs when sellers allows you to *move* the seller financed loan off of the property you purchased and onto another piece of property. This allows you to have a larger equity position on the original property and still gives the sellers an equity position for their collateral. You can use this higher equity position to get a credit line, a development loan or even construction financing. This is a great way for you to raise more capital!

23. Will the seller allow you to *de*-collateralize the loan?

De-collateralization is when an existing loan has a piece of property for collateral and the seller agrees to *release* that property as collateral thereby turning the trust deed and note into a simple *promissory* note. You then own a property free and clear and can do many things with it. This is a very sophisticated way to raise capital though it is quite simple to implement. We will discuss re-collateralization and de-collateralization in much greater detail later in this book.

When you get out in the field and start making offers you'll find many sellers *and* real estate agents may not be familiar with some of the terms with which you are now armed. I have a little advice.

Find out the needs of the seller and make sure they are met first. If you do this, in most cases the seller will go along with whatever else you ask for including such things as seller financing, low interest rates, delayed closings and all of the other formidable terms that can be negotiated.

In Chapter 17 I am going to give you a tool called a "4-offer Spreadsheet". This tool will help you uncover the specific needs of any seller. It also makes it very clear to sellers why they should at least consider offering seller financing. With it your negotiating will be more clear and powerful.

Use these terms and others you learn (or create) to make any deal work for both the buyer *and* seller. Consider these 23 terms when you get any type of seller financing be it, a first lien, second lien or wrap.

CAN A SELLER REALLY FINANCE 100% OF THE PRICE IF THERE IS A LOAN ON THE PROPERTY?
(THE RULES OF WRAPPING)

CAN A SELLER REALLY FINANCE 100% OF THE PRICE IF THERE IS A LOAN ON THE PROPERTY?
(THE RULES OF WRAPPING)

I want to take a little time to go into a bit more detail about the type of seller financing called "wraps". The reason for this is in a slower market, which many areas of the country are experiencing, there is a fantastic opportunity for using this type of financing. It is a fast way to sell a property with inexpensive closing costs. It can be a life saver for someone who has a loan on a property and who must sell fast.

Many of you may have heard you should not wrap a loan. In some cases this is 100% true but in others there is some gray area. I'm here to help you understand how to wrap a loan and take less of a risk. Keep in mind you will find many strategies in this book that don't require wrapping. Don't use this technique if you can't overcome all the obstacles I will be discussing, or if you don't have a good feeling about it. I personally have only wrapped a handful of mortgages in my entire career but when I did, the process worked out extremely well for everyone.

That said, the direct answer to the question, "Can a seller really finance 100 of the price if there is a loan on the property?" is *yes*. There are ways to get 100% financing by the seller even when there is a loan on the property. One way to do it is to 'wrap' the existing mortgage with a new mortgage. Wrapping is an informal way for someone to "assume" a mortgage without permission. There are some pretty big benefits for a buyer to do this. One benefit is the buyer does not have to qualify to assume the loan *or* qualify for a new loan. Also, there are no new loan fees.

If you want to try this technique first talk with a title company or attorney to see if they will help you through the process. If they will and you want to attempt this method here are some tips for you to follow.

First and foremost, check with your state to see if there are any rules or laws against "wrapping" a loan. If not then you can move forward. Make sure the terms of your new loan (the "wrap" or "blanket loan") match the terms of the seller's current loan exactly or at least fairly closely. If there are differences in the underlying mortgage and the wrapped mortgage make sure these differences are in your favor and very small.

For instance you would not want to make a new loan with a seller that will pay off in 10 years if the current loan doesn't pay off for 14 years. The seller would be stuck with a loan and no payments coming in *and no property*. Keep in mind the seller's loan will be on *your* property. In order to avoid this issue, you should sell or refinance relatively soon to pay off the mortgage.

The following are what I call "The Rules of Wrapping". Follow them *every time* you decide to wrap a loan.

"The Rules of Wrapping"

1. If you are worried about wrapping a loan, *don't!* People are worried about wrapping mortgages because of the "Due on Sale" clause we discussed earlier. The fear is the seller's mortgage will be wrapped and the bank will find out and call the mortgage due. This is an important issue to consider. However, given today's economy and the issues in the lending world, banks aren't out

looking for loans on which to foreclose. The amount of properties going to foreclosure is so great most banks are not interested at all in foreclosing on a property where someone is making the payments, and covering the tax and insurance expenses.

2. Never under *any* circumstances, wrap government financing such as FHA and VA loans. Unlike some other loans, government financing has potential penalties to the *buyer* for wrapping it. Other loan types, such as conventional and commercial, typically have no penalties for the *buyer* who wraps those mortgages. Please remember, if something goes wrong there are consequences to a seller who allows a mortgage to be wrapped. Make sure any seller you work with clearly understands this before proceeding with any type of wrap mortgage. Have them read their loan document.

3. Make sure payments are made on time to the seller *and* to the mortgage company. This is best achieved by having a third party accept the buyer's payments, and make the mortgage payment. After the payment is made, everyone is sent a receipt.

4. Get a *new* insurance policy on the property and do *not* cancel the old one. Most insurance payments are covered in the seller's mortgage payment that you will now be paying. If you cancel the insurance policy, the insurance company will notify the mortgage company that the collateral is no longer insured. The mortgage company will start an investigation into this problem.

Make sure you account for this extra expense (of your own insurance policy) when you evaluate your deal. The cost will be insignificant compared to the benefit of this type of financing. By doing this you will make sure the seller's lender and the seller are all covered if something happens. Use *your* insurance if something happens with the property.

5. Make sure all taxes on the property are paid. If the current loan has an escrow account then you should include those amounts when you pay your loan with the seller. This way you pay the taxes to the seller who pays them to the lender. Then, the lender pays them to the taxing authority. Again, if the taxes are not paid, the taxing authority will notify the mortgage company holding the mortgage. The mortgage company will then investigate the situation and potentially call the mortgage due and payable. (Which is their right) Plus if the taxes are not paid the taxing authority may be able to lien the property and foreclose.

6. Only wrap properties for a short time frame. (I recommend one year or less) This is accomplished in the "Foundation to Success" by purchasing the property, putting it immediately back up for sale, creating and enhancing equity in the property by achieving a higher and better use. Once this happens the property will either *sell* for a profit or it will be *refinanced* and you will have an equity position. Either way, the "wrapped" mortgage will be *paid off* in a short period of time.

7. Keep an active financial file open with your lender. My lender always has an up to date financial file on me. That way, if any lender were to call I could very easily submit and get a refinance for a property with a wrapped mortgage. Keeping this up to date file also speeds up the process of getting mortgages for buying any property.

8. Keep private capital connections or a slush fund available at all times. Should a mortgage company call a wrapped mortgage due, you could then very easily pay it off with private capital, or your own funds.

I know you may have more questions about this type of seller financing. If you are unfamiliar with wrapping mortgages it can be quite confusing. Even if you are familiar with it you may still have some big questions. Hang in there! If things seem a bit blurry right now they will soon become quite clear.

BACK-UP PLANS OR....
DROP THAT
DUE ON SALE CLAUSE!

BACK-UP PLANS OR....
DROP THAT
DUE ON SALE CLAUSE!

During the "Wrapping" section of my Camps it is almost a guarantee that someone will come up to the microphone and ask, "What about the "due on sale clause"?

Let me give you some idea about what they are asking. The "due on sale clause" is known in my Camps as the "*don't* on sale clause." I call it that because I usually don't recommend you use "wraps". (Of course there is always an exception to the rule as I will explain later.)

There are so many options to purchase property using your own funds, other people's funds and other forms of seller financing that I consider "wraps" a last resort. That said I'll do my best to explain how the "due on sale clause" works and how you can have a back up plan if a lending institution exercises its right to call the mortgage due.

This well-known "due on sale clause" is what lenders put into a mortgage note which reads something like this, "If the buyer ever sells the mortgaged property the mortgage is to be *paid off* at the time of the sale." In other words, the mortgage is due in full to the mortgage company upon the sale of the property, therefore it is, "due on dale".

The mortgage companies put this clause in to protect themselves from people wrapping their mortgage without permission. The reason for this is the mortgage company had the opportunity to qualify the buyer at the start of the mortgage but not the person who may wrap the mortgage. This leaves the mortgage company vulnerable if an unworthy borrower wraps the loan.

The clause basically says the lender has the right to call the mortgage due and payable if it is discovered that the property has been sold and the mortgage has not been paid in full. The lender can then demand the mortgage be paid in full and if it isn't, has the right to begin foreclosure proceedings on the property

I would like to re-emphasize it is a personal decision whether or not to participate in this kind of financing and you should not do it unless you're willing to accept the associated risks. If you still choose to use this tactic, you should do so with your eyes wide open to the potential pitfalls associated with it. The pitfalls are you may have a lender that calls your note due immediately, or, in some cases you may have broken laws. Stated bluntly, *"Don't* wrap mortgages if you're not prepared for the consequences."

Again, I have wrapped very few mortgages. Not because I couldn't have, but because there are so many other options available when you know all 10 ways to seller finance. You might be thinking you will *never* wrap a mortgage? There is one great exception to my rule. *In an off market you can usually get the lender to drop the due on sale clause! (more on this soon)*

If you decide you want to try a wrap I recommend the following:

- <u>Follow the rules of wrapping</u> in the previous section!

- <u>Get a "Due on Sale Clause" from a lender</u> and review it thoroughly to understand exactly what a lender's perspective and language are in the clause.

- <u>Call a mortgage company</u> and ask them about the practice of wrapped mortgages in general and their perspective on the "Due on Sale Clause". I've had company representatives tell me openly they don't look for problems with loans being paid on time and in full. The fact is the biggest profit from mortgages is made on payments. If a bank borrows money at 3% and loans it to someone else at 6% a handsome profit is made every time a payment is made. Do you really think the bank would want to stop the payments on a mortgage that is being correctly serviced?

- <u>Plan a good exit strategy.</u> This is a back-up plan in case you wrap a mortgage and the loan gets called due and payable. Three of my favorites are:

  i.   <u>Have a refinance package ready</u> at all times with your lender. If the mortgage is called due and payable, the refinance can happen very quickly and the "wrapped" mortgage can be paid off before a foreclosure takes place.

  ii. Make sure you <u>have enough profit</u> in your deal to allow for a handsome discount if you need to sell the property quickly. Cutting the price will help enact a quick sale to pay off the mortgage.

  iii. Have an emergency private lender in place at all times. This will allow you to pay off the called mortgage very quickly with private funds. You'll be able to do this quickly if you get in a pinch.

- <u>Only wrap mortgages on properties that have a "Higher and Better" use.</u> This will allow you to quickly sell for a profit or refinance for an equity position.

- <u>"Create and Enhance Equity"</u> *as fast as possible* after purchase. The sooner you can sell or refinance the less chance there is of a lender calling a note.

- <u>You might consider waiting to record the sale</u> until you are ready to re-sell or refinance. Check to see if this is an option in your state or if you are required to record the change of title immediately.

- <u>Carry a large slush fund</u> to be able to pay off any mortgage that is called due. Some of the investors I know would respond to a due and payable notice with the comment, "Send me wiring instructions and you'll have your mortgage paid off by this time tomorrow."

If you follow these suggestions it will make wrapping mortgages much less risky. As a matter of fact if you follow all of these it is almost risk free. Now let's move onto the exception to the rule where I whole-heartedly think you *should* wrap mortgages!

Over the last couple of years the real estate market has changed dramatically in many parts of the country. Because of the drastic amount of foreclosures on the market there are many lenders that are in high need of people who will service mortgages. In other words, banks and mortgage companies are screaming for anyone to come in and make their loans good by making the payments. Because of this, my absolute favorite way to wrap a loan is to convince the bank or mortgage company to *remove* the "Due on Sale" clause.

Why would a bank ever remove its "Due on Sale" clause? Wouldn't it be taking a huge risk? If you examine the whole picture you will see that not much risk is being taken at all.

When the banks remove the "due on sale" clause they are *not* waiving their right to foreclose if they *aren't paid*. They are just waiving their right to call the note due if the property is *sold*. They are also *not* giving up their collateral position with their mortgage. If the mortgage was in first lien position when the owner got it and the owner sells, that mortgage will still be in first position for the next person in line. In fact, the argument can be made that the longer a mortgage is serviced the more equity will exist behind the mortgage, thereby making banks at less and less risk.

Over the long term the mortgage balance will become lower and the property value will almost always rise. Both of these things make the loan more secure due to the amount of equity behind the indebtedness. So, as long as they are getting the correct timely payments from *someone*, then what is their risk? Isn't their risk higher if they don't remove the clause and have to foreclose on the current owner?

So how are we getting banks to do this? We, meaning my students and I, are calling banks and telling them we want to buy properties and take over payments on the mortgages. At first, banks are saying they could call the loan due. We then ask them, "Do you really need to foreclose on another property? Sometimes banks will even say flat out the mortgages are not assumable. We ask again, "Do you really need to foreclose on another property?"

As the light bulb starts to turn on we explain that they are "the bank" and they have the power to change the loan documents. Once they see the light, banks are either waiving the "Due on Sale" clause in writing making the mortgage legally "wrappable" or in some cases actually adding an assumption clause into the loan for our use. (It is now *"green"*)

I am now taking this a step further and doing what I like to call "Assumptive Short Sales." My students and I are getting lists of properties in pre-foreclosure from banks and mortgage companies. We are then analyzing these lists to find properties with "Higher and Better" uses.

> **Short Sale** – Where the lender agrees to allow the sale of the property when their loan is not paid in full from the proceeds of the sale.
>
> Definition

Once we know which of them fit our investing criteria we call the banks and ask them to allow us to assume the mortgages so foreclosure can be avoided. We agree to assume and make payments if the indebtedness from its current balance can be lowered to the current market value of the property. (or even lower in some cases) We have even been able to get the banks to modify the existing loans in other ways such as lower the interest rate or give us a longer call. In some instances they have just issued new mortgages without even having us qualify. Most banks with foreclosed property on their books will do almost *anything* to avoid having to foreclose on more properties.

One of my students actually called a small bank, talked to the Vice President of lending and requested this technique on a home going into foreclosure. The VP liked it but said the loan was not assumable and the bank couldn't do it. My student countered with, "You're the Vice President, couldn't you just add an assumption clause?" The Vice President remembered the title of VP wasn't just for show and made it happen.

The loan amount was lowered and the existing mortgage was assumed. The seller didn't have to go through a foreclosure; the bank didn't have the hassle and problems and is getting its loan serviced. The buyer picked up great financing in a market where financing is becoming very hard to find.

I suggest you get the list of REO (Real Estate Owned) properties that a bank has, and then tell them you are interested in servicing some of this bad debt. I like to tell a bank I will buy any of the properties on its list that fit my investing criteria if I can *assume* the former loans (or get a new loan with similar or better terms).

I like to get the bank to agree to make the balances at or below market value for the property. The bank must also agree to remove the "Due on Sale" clause and add a simple assumption clause. This market has gotten so bad that investing is really starting to get good! Banks never would have considered this as an option even a year ago, but they do now because of the sheer volume of bad debt and foreclosures in the market place.

The fun thing about this technique is when you get a bank to do this then the loan you have just assumed is now also assumable for the next buyer. If the bank is leery of removing the "Due on Sale" clause for your next buyer, then negotiate! It is smart to do this during due diligence period. Your bank is now the seller and you can offer the bank many of the options we previously discussed concerning seller financing such as:

1. An assumption fee.
2. Required down payment from next buyer.
3. Pay the bank points whenever anyone assumes the loan.
4. Increase the interest rate each time there is an assumption.
5. Increase the loan amount each time the loan is assumed. (Especially if you are doing a short sale where they are lowering the amount of the loan)
6. No further assumptions after the next buyer.
7. Renewable interest-only term. The bank can keep making money forever on the loan.
8. Offer a longer/shorter call or amortization time.
9. Add a prepayment penalty.
10. Additional collateral.
11. Additional cosigners.
12. Minimum credit score.

Use all of your knowledge to get the best deal you can from the bank. You are essentially doing seller financing with the bank. This means all of the terms are up for negotiation!

Now that you know quite a bit more about wrapping a loan, and a new way to create a "green" mortgage, I want to tell you a story. Some time ago I was teaching the topic of wraps to a group of people and one of my students raised his hand and proclaimed, "I don't feel good about wrapping mortgages and I just couldn't do it." I said, "If you feel that way definitely *don't* wrap mortgages. There are risks involved and the technique isn't for everyone."

Several weeks later he came to class and said, "I found a property and wrapped the mortgage and I'm sick about it. I feel so bad about it I can't sleep at night." I asked him why he did it. He said, "I thought it was a good deal." I told him to be sure to make the payments and sell it for a profit or refinance it for an equity position as soon as he possibly could.

The following week he called me and said, "I was so nervous about wrapping the mortgage I called the mortgage company and told them what I did." After I recovered from shock I asked the student what happened. He said, "The bank told me I shouldn't have wrapped the loan and that I will be hearing from them." By this time he was pretty upset.

Just over a week later he received a letter from the bank stating the mortgage *could be* called due and payable at any time. Imagine getting this kind of letter especially when you are already nervous about a transaction. The funny thing is the bank was not saying the mortgage *would be called due*, just that it *could* be.

Over 24 months have passed since the mortgage was wrapped and it has still not been called due. This result is *not* guaranteed, but it shows mortgage companies are in business to make a profit. They do this through the lending of money and the receipt of timely payments, not by calling in their loans.

Wrapping a mortgage is a fantastic way to buy a property and not have the headaches of getting a new loan. Just make sure you cover all of your bases if you attempt this technique, or even better, get the lender to waive the due on sale clause!

Your best move, when using a "wrap", is to get the lender to remove the "Due on Sale" clause!

~Mike Watson

THE "TOP 2" PLACES TO FIND SELLERS WHO ARE RIPE FOR GIVING YOU SELLER FINANCING

(BONUS TOPIC: THE PERFECT STORM)

THE "TOP 2" PLACES TO FIND SELLERS WHO ARE RIPE FOR GIVING YOU SELLER FINANCING
(BONUS TOPIC: THE PERFECT STORM)

There are three main reasons why people or entities more willing to give seller financing. One is they understand how powerful seller financing is for the seller. People will either already know the benefits or you can teach them the benefits.

The second reason people would be more willing to give seller financing is they are having a tough time servicing their debt. The third reason is they are tired of managing their income producing property. I am going to show you how to find people who are tired of property management and/or who are having trouble paying their loans. Let's talk first about those people who are tired of property management.

1. People who have owned multi-family properties for 5 or more years are RIPE for giving you seller financing!

Why is this true? Most sellers who are selling multi-family properties are doing so because they are *tired of property management*. What has happened is, they purchased a property and tried to manage it themselves or had a difficult property management company. Now they are overwhelmed or do not have enough information about the business to make the property profitable and have decided to sell. You need to get to them before they make this final decision. (See my "non-compete" section in my first book, "The Highest and Best Real Estate Investment" for more info.)

One of the reasons these people and their properties are good candidates for investment is this; these owners have realized that when tenants move out there is a huge expense involved with preparing the property again for rental. Also, there is time involved during vacancy and rents are lost. In addition there are marketing costs or commissions to pay. They are now scared of losing tenants so they may over-compensate. Let me explain.

As time passes most owners elect to keep their rents at the current rate so there is less risk of losing tenants. The benefit to you is the *majority* of these properties could handle a rental increase without losing too many tenants. I've increased rents by 20% on a newly purchased apartment complex and have only had one tenant move out.

Another reason why these owners are great to contact about considering seller financing is they understand the power of cash flow. They will respond favorably to the discussion on how their net worth will go up if they provide seller financing. Finally, when you tie it all together, they will be thrilled to have their net worth go up *and* still get cash flow while not having to manage anymore property.

I have students who are contacting every person who has owned a multi-family property for over 5 years in a multiple zip code area in a major metropolitan market. The information they have generated consists of over 1,000 owners who are *ripe* for seller financing.

These students are using what I call "The List". This is a list of information you need to gather about properties. Once you have this list you can narrow down properties in your city or county that fit the criteria for profitable investing (see Step 4 in my 1st book). If you have access, you can give "The List" to a title company and have them create a spreadsheet for you of all the available information. In some states you will be required to pay a small fee for this service. Many times you can get this information from the county tax records. Sometimes this information is just a click of a button away.

"THE LIST"

1. <u>Properties owned for 5+ years.</u> I have mentioned that some potential sellers may be *tired of management* and their properties may have *low rents*. In addition, these properties need to be highlighted because they will most likely *have some equity*. Even though the market has dropped fairly considerably the last year or two, these owners had massive gains when the market was hot. When a property has equity it is easier for the seller to offer seller financing.

The final reason you want to target these owners and properties is if there are loans on the property they are most likely *seasoned*. What I mean by seasoned is payments have been made on them for several years. A seller may have started with a 15 year loan but only has nine years remaining because 6 years worth of payments have already been paid. If you assume this loan you will only have 9 years left and your mortgage payments will pay down the loan quickly.

2. <u>The property address.</u> Obviously this will help you know the locations of the properties and also will enable you to drive by them either prior to or after talking with the owners. Remember, when you are searching tax records for properties you can pull up either the property address or the owner's address. You want both.

3. <u>The owner's mailing address.</u> This is your method of contacting the owner. Typically multi-family units are *not* owner occupied so the *property* address will not help you with finding the

160   *How to Buy and Sell Real Estate without Using a Bank!*

owner. If there is other contact information available, such as phone number, email, P.O. box number, etc., include that as well.

4. <u>The number of units.</u> This will help you narrow down your list. You don't want every property in a county because you won't be able to handle a list that large. I like to have my list include properties with between 4 and 50 units. These are the properties with the highest likelihood of cash flow and also the highest likelihood of being managed by the owner. You could also include duplexes. You will find many people who are self-managing these but your list will possibly be quite long.

5. <u>The lot size.</u> In addition to exploring the current rental potential you will also want to examine properties that may have a potential for a "Higher and Better" use. You might find a 10 unit building on a 2 acre lot that could instead have 20 units on it. This could be a fantastic deal.

Another option is to find properties that could be subdivided. For instance you might find a property listed with a 12 unit building that is actually three 4-plexes. You might be able to subdivide this into 3 lots and sell the 4-plexes separately. They would be worth much more separately than as a single package. (Read all about these techniques in my "The Highest and Best Real Estate Investment" book.)

6. <u>The zoning.</u> Knowing the zoning of a property goes right along with knowing lot size. Right now most city planners are looking for people who will help to re-stimulate and re-vitalize areas within their city. If you offer to go into an area and improve the community, the city may let you increase the density of your property. In addition the zoning will help you know if you can do floor plan changes, square footage additions, etc. (Again see the first book in the series.)

7. <u>Original indebtedness vs. current balance.</u> Usually you can get the *original* loan amount from the purchase through the tax information, but it may be tougher to get the current balance. You could use an amortization schedule to help determine approximately what is owed if you know the original loan amount and date of purchase. This will help you in your negotiations when you find a property to buy.

8. <u>Is the property owned by an LLC or corporation?</u> I have previously discussed the many possibilities when you buy an LLC rather than just a property. This information will trigger ways for you to explore that option. Remember this can be a fantastic way to get pre-existing financing in place for your property.

9. <u>Is the property owned free and clear?</u> When you find a property owned free and clear you can now go after the very best kind of financing. Free and clear seller financing! These sellers may really be tired of managing but may not know what else to do with their equity. Show them how they can make passive property-less income and you may improve their lives dramatically.

My recommendation for you is to get a list of approximately 500 properties which you can narrow down by using zip codes or cities with which you are most familiar. Then you can identify the 50 most important properties designated by the above items. After you have your top 50 properties, create your mailing list of the full 500 but I want you to also *call* the 50.

My students are writing several different letters and sending them out to owners on a periodic basis. In their letters they are asking to talk to owners. In your letters make sure to ask the property owners if they would like to "make more money and never have to manage their property again?" Even if you get a small 3% return on your mailings you are still sitting in front of 15 people a month. These are people you can help.

These are win/win deals staring you in the face. It is time for you to get to work.

FREE Online Resources

We have already created a few sample marketing letters for you to use as a starting point or as a template. You can find these letters our website at **www.mikewatsoninvesting.com/sfbook.**
Click on "Marketing Letters" to get started on writing and sending your letters!

One exciting technique I've used when talking to a multi-family unit owner is offering them more monthly income than they are making right now. This is an amazing way to get owners of income property to sell their property and offer seller financing. This is especially true when they own the property outright. Let me show you an example of how this works.

Let's assume a seller, Mr. X, owns a 4-plex "free and clear" and it is worth $400,000. This property is currently rented at $600 for each unit. That means Mr. X is making $2400 in gross rent per month. That is a "gross operating income" (GOI) of $28,800 per year ($2400 x12). In order to figure an approximate "net operating income" (NOI) multiply the GOI by 70% totaling $20,160. ($28,800 x .7) I use this to show an *approximate* expense of 30% of the total gross rents. (This includes things like taxes, insurance, and maintenance.)

So in this example the NOI is $20,160 per year. If you divide the NOI by $400,000 (The value of the property) it gives you the owner's percentage return on the property. In this case their return is 5.04%! ($20,160/$400,000=.0504)

If you buy this property and are given a $400,000 loan with 6% interest-only payments Mr. X will make $24,000 which is a 20% increase over the old NOI! He will make more money by selling the property than keeping it! There is more cash flow and no property management. Do you see why this is a great reason to sell? What if you were offered to pay 7% interest? Could you use this as a tool to convince sellers to sell to you with 100% seller financing? (I bet you could.)

But why would *you* want to buy this property? Your debt service and expenses could be more than your rental income. Here is the key. Only use this technique on a property where you are going to *increase the value of the property by increasing one of the types of density.*

Usually I use this technique on a property where I know the rents are low, the vacancy is high or I can eliminate or lower some of my expenses. Some options to increase the density might be to add units, square footage, or even laundry or covered parking. By increasing density in these ways I make up for the discrepancy in my rents versus payments very quickly. Find those multi-family owners and start making deals!

Next let's explore our 2nd place to find seller financing deals. I am going to show you how to find banks that are desperate to offer you seller financing. Yes, you read that right. Read on!

2. Banks (Credit Unions and Mortgage Companies) are RIPE for offering you seller financing!

I have already mentioned that banks are starting to allow people to assume loans by dropping the due on sale clause. Now, why would I say that banks are ripe for *seller financing?* Any bank with an REO (Real Estate Owned) property list has debt that is not being serviced at all. (Loans that aren't being paid) Therefore they need someone who can service that debt otherwise it hurts their power to lend out money.

I have talked about approaching banks briefly but here is the key, you must talk to the right person. Let's go through how that will work and let me give you a couple of things you can bring to the discussion.

A few of my students are calling every bank in their area and asking to speak with the head of the commercial lending department. If they get connected directly to this department, the discussion starts like this, "I am an investor and am working with a group of people who specialize in taking bad debt off the books of banks. We are happy to look at *any* property you have and can move very quickly."

If an assistant or "gate keeper" has answered the phone then usually they will try to stall the student from getting to the decision maker. If this happens the student states up front, "My associates and I have a list of about 62 questions that need clarification so get a pen and lots of paper!" Then the student begins giving criteria of properties they are willing to buy. Soon the assistant says, "Wait! I'll get you the head of the department".

The point of this discussion with a bank is to get your hands on its list of REO properties. Then let the bank know you are willing to buy any property it is willing to finance that meets your criteria!

In other words, this means you might be interested in buying some of those properties *IF* they will let you assume any of the loans on the properties, possibly at a lower loan value, *or* if they will finance the property for you.

If you find out the bank has REO's but isn't willing to discuss the financing, tell the bank, "You already did finance it, I just want to service some of that bad debt". That might get their attention.

One of the things you need to determine is whether or not the bank carries its own loans. That is, does it sell or keep its loans? If the loans are sold, there probably won't be an REO list. If the loans are kept however, the bank may very well be quite excited to talk with you.

Use all of your negotiating tactics with the bank as if it was an individual seller. Have some fun! Find some awesome deals with incredible "Higher and Better" uses and make some great profits, equity positions, and cash flows! Remember, if there is not a "Due on Sale" clause then you can also offer that property as a wrap to the next buyer.

Why Banks Are Seller Financing
(and don't tell them I told you about it)

Many people in America believe we are having a real estate crisis. I believe we are having a *lending* crisis. If banks would lend more, real estate would start moving again. However, many banks are faced with one big problem….. they have *no money* to lend to borrowers no matter how qualified those buyers might be. And even worse, the bank can't even borrow money to make loans.

Let me explain why these two things are true. The bad debt that banks are dealing with now is really causing a problem for them. Consider the following list of repercussions to banks that have foreclosed loans on their books.

1. Banks are required by the FDIC (The Federal Deposit Insurance Corporation insures people's deposits at banks) to carry a percentage of cash on hand for all bad debt that they have in their lending portfolios. This means they have to put cash in reserve that they could lend to borrowers as a security against their bad debt. (Right now banks don't have any cash reserves.)

2. Typically a bank can borrow up to 5-7 times the amount of its deposits from the Federal Reserve for lending purposes. If it has bad debt then this is not allowed. This means that if I am a bank or mortgage company that has $100 million in bad debt, this could stop me from borrowing up to $500-$700 million dollars to lend to my current and future customers. (Right now banks can't borrow any money because of the bad debt on their books.)

You can find out more information on both #1 and #2 at FDIC.com

3. When a borrower stops making payments on a bank's loan, the bank still has to make a payment to the place where it borrowed the money (if it was borrowed funds, which is usually the

case). This situation is very similar to owning a 4-Plex with non-paying tenants in it. You would still have to pay the mortgage even though you weren't getting the income to which you were entitled. Think how much a bank would have to pay on $100 million dollars of foreclosed loans if it is still paying interest on these loans. (Right now it has no income but it still has expenses.

4. When a bank takes back a property, (which is costly with attorney's fees) it not only loses the payment from the former borrower, and has to service the interest payment it has on that debt, it still has to *take care of the foreclosed properties*. Property taxes, insurance, utilities and other expenses still must be paid by the bank.

5. As a bank's bad debt or Real Estate Owned (REO) portfolio increases its stock prices drop considerably. One of the ways a bank will raise capital for lending purposes is to sell its stock. If the stock won't sell and it is low in value, it is hard for a bank to raise capital. (Right now a bank can't borrow or raise capital.)

6. If enough of these things happen, the bank will run the risk of not being federally insured by the FDIC and it may have to close down. (Now you are probably getting a much clearer picture of what is happening with the banks in the US.)

Because of the above list, banks aren't lending. They don't have money to lend, they can't raise money to lend and things are just getting worse. This is why when you go into a bank and ask for a loan you are told "No". Eventually you will get some really creative reason so it will seem as if the problem lies with you, but most of the rejections, especially for qualified buyers, are because there is no money to lend. Banks won't tell you this because they don't want the public to know that they have no money. Here is how I learned these things.

Very recently I went to a large Midwestern bank to get some documents from my safe deposit box. I had to wait longer than normal to get into my box because a group of individuals were in the branch president's office in a meeting.

When they saw me waiting, one lady hurried over and apologized for making me wait. She told me they were in an important meeting trying to figure out how to raise the number of accounts and deposits in their bank. (Accounts are assets while deposits are cash on hand. Having these two things will allow them to borrow more money from the Federal Reserve and make loans to consumers for profits.) This is the only way they will survive!

I angrily replied, "You should be more worried about losing deposits from unhappy customers than getting new customers." She asked why I was upset. I explained that I had been a fantastic customer to them for 15 years and had flawless credit and history with the bank. I had correctly serviced all my credit lines, commercial loan accounts and other things the bank had set up for me. But now the bank won't lend to me anymore. I was preparing to take my seven deposit accounts (which held considerable average daily balances) and go to another bank that wanted to lend to me. She didn't say much more so I continued into the safe deposit box area.

When I came out, the bank Vice President asked if I would step into a meeting with him and the bank President. I told them of my frustrations. The bank President looked me straight in the eye and told me the bank had no money to lend. I was shocked that they were willing to admit this to me. They promised to set up a meeting with a regional commercial VP to see what could be done. Banks aren't lending because in most cases *there is no money to lend.*

Why is this important in a seller financing book? Obviously, the reason is that most banks won't give you a loan. However, if you find *bank owned* assets and tell the bank you will buy every property it owns that meets your criteria it's almost guaranteed the bank will work with you. The bank will lend to you all day long. (Because it can!)

Why can you get a loan from the bank on assets it owns but not on anything else? This is because the bank foreclosed on the properties that are now in the bank's Real Estate Owned schedule. Even though it may have borrowed the money for the first loan, the properties now have come back from the foreclosure auction *free and clear.*

Because of this the bank doesn't need to have any *cash on hand* to make me a loan on *this* property! When the bank owns a property free and clear it can loan to anyone and can work out *any* terms for the financing. It can finance the property because it is the SELLER. All it has to do is create the loan documents. It doesn't have to bring cash to the closing to pay the seller because it *is* the seller.

A bank would probably never consider this as being seller financing because it is usually in the business of lending money. Now, however, it has become the *seller* and is issuing financing. This is the textbook definition of seller financing!

If a bank will offer me seller financing, then it doesn't have to go get cash to give me a loan on one of these properties. It also has now *freed up cash held in reserve* for this bad debt. It can borrow more money from the Federal Reserve Bank and is now *receiving income* usually over and above the debt payment for what was borrowed on this property. In addition someone else is paying for the expenses of the property. (Taxes, insurance, maintenance, management) Stock prices and financial reporting look better. This whole process significantly decreases the chance of having the bank shut down as its bad debt becomes good debt again. Seller financing can even save the banks!

There are so many reasons why a bank should seller finance to you. Even though this is the case, you should never go into a bank and say, "Will you seller finance some of your property to me?" A bank won't handle this well at all. It might not have any idea about what you are proposing.

However, you *should* say, "I will buy any property you own in your Real Estate Owned Schedule that you will finance for me as long as it meets my investing criteria." Talk about saying the magic words! If you are talking to the right person, you will have their undivided attention. Banks, mortgage companies and credit unions are all great places to practice this technique.

Banks are so interested in getting rid of their bad debt that they are including some crazy terms along with the sales of these properties. My students and I have obtained the following terms using bank seller financing:

1. Extremely low interest rates (2, 3, 4%).
2. No interest payments or principal only loans.
3. Interest only payments.
4. Quarterly, semi-annual or annual payments.
5. Assumable loans.
6. Loans to brand new LLCs.
7. Loans without tax returns or credit scores being provided.
8. Property purchases with construction financing agreed upon for the future project on the property.
9. Little or no money down.
10. Assumptive Short Sales on previous loans.

The sky is the limit. It is in the banks' best interest to get rid of this bad debt. It is in your interest to buy with low prices and fantastic terms!

Let's put our two main concepts together. First you want to find people with multi-family properties that have been owned for five or more years. Contact these people and find out who is tired of managing. Buy these properties using seller financing terms that make the deal work for everyone.

In addition you want to find people who own properties like these, who may be heading toward or who are in foreclosure. This may be best achieved by talking directly with banks. Let's look at why there are going to be more and more of these multi-family properties available to buy.

Why Income Producing Properties
Are Foreclosing
(and thereby being made available
for bank seller financing)

Historically when there are lots of foreclosures the vast majority of properties that get foreclosed are single family, owner occupied homes. This is true because when people lose their source of income they typically end up losing their home. Usually *income producing* properties can support themselves thus avoiding foreclosure. In today's market we are seeing an alarming trend. Multi-family income producing properties are facing foreclosure in record numbers.

These multi-family properties are going into foreclosure because the economy is so bad that investors are actually *taking the rents from their buildings and living on them* instead of making their investment's mortgage payments. Owners are essentially saying that they will strip their income producing properties of rents (which will be used to live on) so they can forestall losing their own homes. As a result, these multi-family properties are being lost to foreclosure and if things don't turn around the owners homes will also eventually be lost.

My favorite kind of income producing property to buy, especially in a foreclosure market, is the apartment complex that provides entry level rental units. Why are these properties going to be such a great deal? And why is this setting up to be the "Perfect Storm" for investing?

"The Perfect Storm"

First and foremost, the national trend analysis usually shows increased occupancy in apartments during times when the housing market dips. Some of the reasons for this in today's market are:

1. With the real estate market in disarray, builders aren't building new housing inventory because people aren't buying. (Fewer new homes)

2. Banks aren't lending on existing new inventory because of the numbers of foreclosures.

3. New apartment housing complexes are not being built to support growth due to fear of the economy and banking crisis. (No new apartments)

4. Net immigration is still up in most major metropolitan markets without significant increases in housing for these people. (More renters coming to U.S.)

5. The "echo boomers" are coming! Over the next ten years an expected 70 million children of the baby boomers are going to be coming of rental age. (More demand for rental units)

6. Large numbers of former homeowners are being pushed back into the rental market. (Foreclosure = no buying, therefore, must rent)

7. The trend is still towards single residence families moving into two residence families because of divorces. When a couple divorces, additional housing is needed and therefore demand is increased.

Online Resources

I found a great resource for statistics and analysis of the national housing market. Harvard University's Joint Center for Housing Studies publishes a report called, "The State of the Nation's Housing".
You can download these reports for free at **www.jchs.harvard.edu**.

With less units of inventory (supply) and more people needing rental units (demand) the rents will be pushed *up* in many areas. Amazingly we are seeing a *downward* trend of the prices and values of income producing property at the same time these rents are rising. What happens when you meld these two outcomes is that it improves cash flow from the property.

Right now my students and I are buying income producing properties in many areas of the United States at less than 40 cents on the dollar compared to prices just two years ago. The incredible news is that most of the rents on these properties are 20% or higher *now* than they were at that time. Can you believe we are finding nearly half the price along with more rental income? What a time to buy!

The banks are selling multi-family income properties in record numbers. Imagine buying these properties right now at huge discounts, with incredible terms and increasing rents. Banks want to get rid of these properties because of the bad debt it creates on their books. Also, there are additional expenses involved to hold onto these properties.

Finally, banks are not equipped to manage property. They tend to lose a lot of tenants during their time of ownership. The incredible opportunity for us is that when the occupancy drops, the price goes down with it. This is truly "A Perfect Storm" for investing in income producing real estate! Talk to these lenders, scour their bad debt for income producing properties and go after them!

FOUR OTHER PLACES TO FIND SELLERS WHO ARE RIPE FOR OFFERING YOU SELLER FINANCING

FOUR OTHER PLACES TO FIND SELLERS WHO ARE RIPE FOR OFFERING YOU SELLER FINANCING

There are four other places you can find a significant amount of sellers who are willing to give you seller financing. First you can search properties that are currently for sale through real estate agents. Next, "For Sale By Owner" properties usually are a big sign saying, "I need help!" Another good source is to go directly to an owner rather than the bank when you obtain a "Notice of Default" list. Next you should aggressively approach owners who are offering their properties for sale as a lease-purchase. Let me explain these in more depth.

1. Properties listed with an agent:

This option may sound a little generic. I'm not saying here that every home or property listed with an agent offers a good opportunity for finding a seller interested in seller financing. What I am going to do is give you a tool to help you sift through to find those owners who *are* interested.

The first thing to do is decide what type of deal is best for you. If you have no idea you should refer to my first book. It helps you determine a type of property you want for investment. The focus is always to find a property with a "Higher and Better" use than it currently is using. (Remember you want more density and, any one of the five types is great! Units, Tax ID's, Square Footage, Income and/or Terms)

Once you have a list of properties with a "Higher and Better" use you are going to send the listing agents a letter, fax or email. This communication will have the following statement, "I would make an offer on your listing if your seller is willing to ...." Finish this with a list of items that mainly represent "seller financing" without actually saying "will you seller finance to me?" (Well, you say it once just in case they are openly interested.) The reason you want to send this list to the agents is to get their attention. In a rough market any agents "worth their salt" will follow up on *any* lead they that could possibly result in a buyer for their listings. Here is how your communication will read:

"I will make an offer on your listing if your seller is willing to do one or more of the following items ...."
1. Consider terms for payment.
2. Allow the buyer to assume or wrap the mortgage.
3. Allow a longer closing period on the contract.
4. Consider another property in trade.
5. Partner with me for a profit.
6. Take a large sum of money at closing and more money later.
7. Be willing to receive 2 or 3 times your asking price over time.
8. Consider seller financing.
9. Consider making part of the monthly payment.
10. Carry some of the equity as a 2nd lien.
11. Make seller financing assumable under agreed upon circumstances.
12. Allow work or access to the property prior to an extended closing date.
13. Allow city processes such as zone changes, site plans and

plat maps to start during an extended closing time.

14. Take income over time.

15. Delay their capital gains taxes.

16. Like to have passive income without property management.

17. Like to pay small taxes over time rather than one lump sum.

18. Have a quick closing combined with anything listed from 1-17.

19. Get a higher sales price than the market value.

20. Like to become a better investor.

Why would you use this list? Sometimes there is a bit of a stigma and fear around seller financing and you have to overcome this by educating sellers (and real estate agents). These items are ways of describing seller financing which are much more subtle and if one or more of these things are interesting enough, you may get a return call and will then have hooked a good fish on your line for seller financing.

2. Properties that are "For Sale By Owner"

Many times owners will try to sell their property without a real estate agent when they are having trouble with their finances. They may be having a hard time making their payments or they may not have enough equity to pay a real estate agent a commission.

They are in a bit of a pinch. You are now armed with enough tools to help them. Call every "For Sale by Owner" you find. Talk with them and help them, using all the techniques of seller financing you have now learned. If the property is a good deal buy it! If you are a real estate agent either buy it or help sell the property using seller financing. It can only help the market to have more sales and fewer foreclosures!

3. NOD Lists

A NOD list is a something that names the people in a certain area that have been given a "Notice of Default" on their loan. These people are having an absolutely terrible time with their payments. They have already defaulted on their loan and the lender has started the foreclosure process. Remember, people in this position will usually be more open to seller financing if it will help them escape this situation.

Many times title companies will have lists of the Notices of Default. In addition you may be able to get this information from your county tax authority or your courthouse. Once you have this list determine the properties that meet your investing criteria. Next, go talk to the owners of these properties and see if there is any way they are able to seller finance to you. If you can save them from having a foreclosure on their record you will be doing them a huge favor. This group of people is also ripe for short sales and assumptive short sales.

4. Properties for sale as Lease Purchase or Lease Option

Typically when you find a property for sale offering a lease option the seller is having a hard time selling the property. This type of sale is usually used as a last resort.

There are two types of people who offer to give a lease purchase. The first is the person having a hard time selling; the second is someone who wants to take advantage of potential buyers. These sellers are rare but they are out there, so beware.

This second type never really wants to consummate a sale. The sale is only being offered in this way to get someone to pay them a deposit *and* a higher than market rent. These sellers know that over 90% of the people who enter into this type of agreement will never be able to buy the property. They are happy with this because they just want to take the "buyer's" money and start all over again. These types are easy to spot because they will be unwilling to seller finance their property to you because this would be an actual sale.

The following discussion assumes you are dealing with the first type of seller; the one who is having a hard time selling. These people really do want to sell and can be converted to a seller finance sale very easily. Let me show you how a lease option works and then show you how to get the seller to consider seller financing instead.

How a Lease Option or Lease Purchase Works

Sellers usually require a larger deposit, or "option" deposit and higher-than-market rent. Later the deposit can usually become part of the purchase and the higher-than-market rent can have a small monthly portion credited to the buyer for their potential purchase.

Buyers are typically interested in a lease option when they are not financially prepared to purchase a home right now. In setting up a lease option buyers get the following benefits:

1. A fixed purchase price for a predetermined rental period of time. The hope is that the price the contract was fixed at will be lower than market value when the option ends. This will allow the buyer to purchase a property under the current market value.

2. A monthly rent that usually includes a portion of the payment as a future gift or concession by the seller towards the buyer's closing costs or down payment for the purchase.

3. Time to get their purchase credit, income, job history and loan application in order so that they qualify for the loan.

Sellers will usually offer their property for lease option because they can't sell it traditionally in the current market place. Benefits to sellers include:

1. A higher quality tenant - This tenant is going to try and buy the property later and therefore has a desire to take better care of the property.

2. Higher Monthly Rents - The seller charges higher monthly rents and then offers a portion of it back to the renters on the condition they purchase the property at a later date. If the renters don't buy the home, then the sellers keep the higher-than-market rents as extra profit.

3. A larger deposit - The renters put down a larger deposit because they can use it later as part of a down payment on the purchase of the property. The seller likes this because if the buyer doesn't perform they have a renter with a larger deposit at stake. Sometimes sellers keep the entire deposit and consider it a lost option fee for the buyer.

4. A tenant that will stay longer - Tenants can be fairly transient. If tenants sign a two or three year lease with the intent to buy the property at the end, the chances are good that they will stay for that period of time.

Now that we think lease options sound like a good idea for both parties, let's consider reality. *The vast majority of lease options entered into as leases never end up as purchases.* The reasons include:

1. The tenants may not have improved their credit, job history, debt or other issues that kept them from getting a loan in the first place.

2. More than likely the buyers will not have a large enough down payment to make it work. This is because the rent they

were paying was a larger rent than current market. The portion that was credited to them from the seller along with the down payment earned through the rental deposit usually doesn't total more than three or four percent of the future purchase price. This isn't enough to buy the house.

3. If the home has increased in value, the difference between the value of the home and the purchase price doesn't help buyers. If a buyer has a lease option price of $300,000 and the market value of the home at the time they want to buy is $335,000, the $35,000 of "equity" in the property does not in any way help the buyer. They still have to put down the same amount of money even though the appraisal will be much higher.

4. The value of the property may have dropped during the lease option term and may now be worth less than the tenant buyer's price for a purchase. No one wants to buy a property that is up-side down in value at the time they buy it. No lender will loan on this type of property. It won't have a high enough appraisal value which is required by lenders.

The sad reality with this program is that there is usually a buyer who wants to buy and a seller who wants to sell. Unfortunately this program rarely helps anyone buy or sell a property. So, let's look at how we can consummate a sale.

How can you get sellers to agree to seller finance when they are offering a lease option?

When I first started thinking about lease options I approached a seller who wanted to sell a property and couldn't, so she was offering it as a lease option.

During our meeting about the property she was telling me about her terms. The thought occurred to me that the terms of the lease option sounded an awful lot like the terms I would put together in a seller financed deal. Plus if I worked out a seller financed deal she would have a much better chance of actually selling the property and getting paid her equity. Let's look at the terms of a lease option and see how they compare to a seller financed transaction.

1. The option deposit could be the same amount and now *would* be a down payment in the form of earnest money.

2. The monthly rent could easily be turned into a monthly mortgage payment on a loan amortized over 30 years.

3. The lease option period could easily become a call period (time when the loan is due and payable to the seller). If the lease option was for three years, the seller would be hoping to get the money from their sale in three years. If a buyer bought the home and had a balloon or call in three years and *refinanced* the loan instead of purchasing the home at that point, the seller would still get her money at the same time.

4. In fact, allowing the buyer to purchase the home and have his or her name on the title would actually improve the chances of the seller getting her money in three years. That is because if the home went up in value from $300,000 to $335,000 the buyer would have $35,000 in *equity* now in addition to the original down payment plus any principal reduction in the three years of mortgage payments. This vastly improves the chance that the buyer will be able to refinance the property and pay off the seller's loan.

These subtle differences sounded to me like a much better deal for everyone. I excitedly approached the seller about seller financing. I showed her how to sell the property now and receive her proceeds in three years with a refinance. I explained the "Foundation to Success" and that as the owner I could either sell the property for a profit and pay off her loan or refinance the property after changing the property to its "Highest and Best Use". Either way she would get paid.

The seller's odds of getting paid were much higher with me buying instead of going the lease option route with a different person. If the seller was serious about getting paid, she would really consider this option. (She ended up doing the deal.)

After several more meetings with the owner and a few more deals like this my presentation evolved into a couple of simple questions. These questions cause almost every seller to be willing to offer seller financing instead of offering just a lease option.

The first question to ask sellers is, "Would you like to significantly increase your chance of selling your property and receiving your money?" This is a powerful question. How can any sellers answer "no" to this question? When they answer "yes" I explain the reasoning and they usually understand very quickly why the seller financing option is a better choice.

If they aren't convinced then the second question to ask is, "Would you like your money sooner?" Again, this is a powerful question that few sellers can say no to. If the lease option term was going to be three years, you might offer a seller finance purchase with a 30 year amortized loan that has a two and a half year call. This would mean the seller would get their proceeds 6 months earlier.

I suggest you negotiate a long term for the call time. That is because in most cases you will be doing something to the property to make it more valuable. These changes will take time. In my experience they always take more time than you think. Give yourself enough time to make the property worth more so you can sell or refinance it without worrying about when the loan is due.

Another technique you can use is to settle all of the terms the seller wants for the lease option. Then, offer to match those terms but turn them into seller financing terms and close in seven days. Believe me; you will have their attention, especially if their property has been on the market for any length of time.

I did this on a property very early in my career. A gentleman had a duplex for sale that had horrible tenants. They were not paying him rent at all. He was in a very distressed situation as he still had a mortgage payment but no rents.

During our discussions I asked him what his terms were for his lease purchase and then I offered to take over his mortgage now instead. (Seller finance wrap). He was so thrilled that I was going to solve his problem that we signed the offer right there and I only gave him $1 earnest money deposit.

After the purchase was completed I got those tenants out, got the property rented properly, enjoyed a handsome cash flow on it for a couple of years and then sold it for a nice profit. The seller, on the other hand, had someone else make his payments and then received his equity in two years. Both of us were very happy!

> Owners who have their property for sale as "Lease-Purchase" are a simple step away from seller financing!
>
> **~Mike Watson**

HOW TO GET THE SELLER TO "SEE THE LIGHT"

HOW TO GET THE SELLER TO "SEE THE LIGHT"

At this point you are probably chomping at the bit to do some seller financing. Unfortunately your excitement is only one side of the equation. How do you get the seller to feel the same way? I've mentioned a couple of ideas in other sections but in this chapter I want to show you how to handle some of the other objections you may encounter from sellers.

How do you get the seller excited about offering seller financing to you? The answer to this question is *you* must take the time to *understand seller financing* and then you must take the time to *explain the benefits to the sellers.*

Most people do not understand why seller financing is so valuable. When you understand why it is such an incredible tool and then present your "4-offer spread sheet" it will usually become clear to *them* why seller financing is a phenomenal opportunity. (4-offer spreadsheet coming soon)

Even with all this information you may still run into some resistance. Over the years I've noticed a few basic reasons why sellers are leery of seller financing.

Here are the objections you may run into and some effective ways to handle them.

Reasons against seller financing	Your Solution
1. Sellers don't understand why the property should be financed.	*Educate* the sellers using the list of benefits.
2. The sellers don't trust you.	You can offer to give them other properties as collateral, have co-signers, or pay a higher interest rate, etc. Find out what will make them feel comfortable and give it to them if it is reasonable. You can offer the first few months of payments as earnest money or offer to pay a few months up front at closing.
3. They want proof you qualify for the payments	See #2
4. They worry you won't take care of the property	Talk to them about how you will create or enhance equity and how that will *increase* the value of the property.
5. They worry about you making little or no down payment.	Put a down payment in a trust account to prove you have cash.

6. They are worried about their capital gains tax.	Let them know they won't have to pay until they realize the returns. (Have them check with a CPA familiar with real estate issues)
7. They need the down payment for their next home.	Let them stay in the property during the call time. They can rent from you. You may only need to do this for 6-12 months.
8. Sellers think they won't qualify for another home.	Same as #6, plus remember your payements to them count as income.
9. They are worried about the "Due on Sale Clause".	Don't cancel their insurance, pay taxes and make sure the payment is made. (See "Rule of Wrapping" section.)
10. They are concerned about the loss of tax advantages	Increased income and no property management offsets the tax advantages. (Check with their cpa.)

Over the years I have noticed there is no way to predict every objection sellers will have about doing seller financing. On the other hand, you can use one of the following four solutions to calm their fears with about 95% of the objections you will hear.

1. Occupancy:

Have them stay in the property until you pay them off. That way the sellers won't have to get a new loan for another property until this one is paid off. In addition they can make sure the property is cared for since they will be the one's living there.

An example of this would be if you are buying someone's home and they give you a loan that has a one year call time. Have them live there for the one year until you pay them off with a sale or refinance. This allows you to do things to the property like platting, zoning and subdivisions and their rent pays the mortgage. They will feel like the property is being taken care of because they are living there.

2. Term of call or balloon (the amount of time until they will be paid in full):

Don't do *long-term* seller financing. If you keep the balloon time frame under a year or two, the sellers will feel more comfortable. Very few sellers will want to seller finance for a full 30 years unless you are buying their income producing property and they want the continued cash flow.

Most seller financed properties can easily be sold or refinanced within 180 days of closing as long as there are significant alterations that "Create and Enhance Equity." (If you are buying a multi-family unit where there are not any immediate ways to increase the value this solution may not work, but again sellers may be more interested in having a longer term note.)

3. Collateralization of other real property:

This is your promise that, "If I don't make my payments to you not only can you take the property back; you can take *another* property, too!" This gives the seller recourse that can be extremely painful to you. You should of course, *always* make your payment.

Another way to use this technique is to use another property as a down payment using a note. For example, you might buy a $500,000 property with a $500,000 Trust Deed and Note on the subject property and then put a second note for $50,000 on another piece of property you own. This would be equal to a reasonable down payment on the first property. Always make sure language in the first loan releases the second loan when it is paid in full so you don't end up paying $550,000 for your mortgages.

4. Additional Co-signers:

There is implied strength in numbers. What would sellers say if you told them, "I'll have 14 people sign on your loan and share the responsibility for repayment"? They would most likely be thrilled that they can go after 14 people if payments aren't made. And, if any of those people have significant assets and worth, their signature may be a more valuable piece of collateralization than a piece of property. One benefit for you and your co-signers is that a seller financed mortgage does not appear on the co-signers' credit reports.

If after you have explained all of the benefits and attempted to ease the sellers' minds you are still unable to get them to offer seller financing, the last option is to attempt to get an *extended closing*. This in itself is a form of seller financing, as previously explained.

FREE Online Resources

I have a FREE audio clip of a "role play" demonstrating how to talk with a seller about seller financing, and how to overcome their objections.
Go to **www.mikewatsoninvesting.com/sfbook** and click on "Seller Finance Role Play Audio" to get a sampling of how to explain seller financing in a way that will show the incredible benefits to be received from offering seller financing.

If you explain seller financing correctly almost every seller will be willing to offer you seller financing!

~Mike Watson

Let's move on to the next tool you can use to help sellers understand the benefits they receive by offering seller financing.

POWER OF THE
"4-OFFER SPREADSHEET"

CHAPTER **17**

POWER OF THE "4-OFFER SPREADSHEET"

At this time I would like to share another intriguing example of seller financing from one of my students. Julie was the type of investor who loved to create win/win deals. She had been actively contacting sellers with her non-compete campaign. (See my "Highest and Best Real Estate Investment Book, Step #3.)

One day Julie was meeting with a man who had called her about selling his property. He had a duplex he wished to sell because he lived out of town and it was becoming difficult to manage. She was very interested in buying the property. She had already done her complete deal evaluation (See my "Highest and best Real Estate Investment Book, Step #4) and knew this would be a fantastic property to change into its "Highest and Best" use. (She was going to increase the density by doing a condo conversion and therefore having two owners rather than one.)

To make a long story short, Julie was showing the seller the "4-offer spreadsheet". He turned to her and said, "Is there any way I can give you seller financing on *all* of my equity?" You see, Julie's spreadsheet had shown the seller he could get cash for the property, or he could finance a *portion* of his equity. It did not have an option where he financed *all* of his equity.

Julie was a little thrown off but very excited. She said, "Of course, let's look at how much equity you have in the property". She went on to find out that the seller had a loan for $155,000 on the property. She was offering him $325,000 as a purchase price. He was so interested in doing seller financing that he financed all of his equity. The fact that he financed every penny of his equity may not seem significant except he actually *brought money* to the closing to pay for his closing costs in order to do so.

Why in the world would he want to do this? First, he believed Julie would make all of her payments. (Which she did, and still is) Second, he saw the light. He realized that the income stream created by offering seller financing would be a fantastic change in his life. He wanted to get as much per month as he could. Smart move Mr. Seller!

Here is how this looked at closing. Julie got a loan from a bank for $155,000. This loan paid off the original loan the seller had on the property. The bank did not require Julie to put any money down because her loan was so small compared to the value of the property appraised subject to the condo conversion. Then the seller gave Julie a loan for $170,000.

Julie came to the table with very little money. There were about $500 of closing costs and that was it. Julie then changed the use of the property and increased its value by almost $100,000. She then sold the property and made a nice profit. (We will talk about this seller in a later section. Keep him in mind.)

This is a fantastic example of how you can use seller financing to raise the capital you need to buy a property. The major point of this story is the "4-offer spreadsheet" because it was the tool that showed the seller his different options and possible profits with each option. Here is how the "4-offer spreadsheet" works.

The "4-Offer Spreadsheet"

What is this notorious "4-offer spreadsheet"? It is a spreadsheet you present to seller that shows four different offers on their property. I talk about the "4-offer spreadsheet" at length in my book, "The Highest and Best Real Estate Investment". I am going to go over it again in this book but am going to add a twist. In book #1, I use the

"4-offer spreadsheet" to open up negotiations with sellers to find out their needs. This is still how it is used but for your eyes only the twist is this; *the entire reason to make more than one offer is to get sellers to be your bank!* In other words it is to get them to give you some seller financing.

The way a simple "4-offer spreadsheet" can accomplish this coveted result is by showing sellers how much MORE money they can make by financing their equity to you than just by selling the property outright. Let's take a deeper look at this spreadsheet. Here is a small section from book #1 followed by the twist:

It's time to make an offer! Or should I say, it's time to make *four* offers. This doesn't mean make four offers on four properties. I'm saying you are going to make four offers on *one* property.

Why would you make four offers on one property? Because you want to determine the seller's needs. It is very important to determine what these are prior to going under contract. Once you have established the seller's needs you will know *exactly* how to negotiate.

Typically sellers will tell you they have many needs. But the truth is that most sellers only have two or three main needs when they sell their property. Once you determine those critical needs then you can *fulfill the needs of the sellers* and then manipulate the other terms to *your* benefit. This is a powerful concept when you consider all the terms we have discussed so far in this book. (Remember the "Top 23" terms...)

Here is just one example of how this works. If sellers want to have their money very *fast* you can negotiate a lower price. If all they care about is getting *full* price then you can negotiate a later closing date or a lower interest rate on the seller financing.

How exactly does making four offers tell you what the sellers need? When you make multiple offers sellers can decide which terms will or will not work for them. If you make sure *all* of the offers work for *you* by manipulating the terms, the sellers may be more flexible and then you can create a win/win situation at the end of your negotiations.

The easiest way to make four offers at once is to create a spreadsheet of the four offers on one page. That way it is a simple presentation and has a more powerful impact. Here is a description of one I've taught my students to use followed by the actual spreadsheet. You can modify it to fit each of your transactions.

Here is a synopsis of the different offers on the spreadsheet:

Offer #1 is an "all cash" offer.

The first offer you have on your spreadsheet is an "All Cash" offer. It is also your lowest offer. Cash carries with it a cost. If you are using your own cash you will be foregoing the interest you otherwise could have made on that cash. If you are using someone else's cash you will have to pay them an interest rate on the money. You cannot afford to pay cash unless you are somehow compensated for that cost through the price.

You should always include a cash offer on your spreadsheet. This is whether or not you have the cash on hand. There are two reasons for this. Number one is that when you offer cash you give sellers a feeling of confidence. They think, "If this person can pay cash for the property then obviously there isn't a whole lot of risk in seller financing." You want sellers to have confidence in you.

The second reason you offer cash is that if you are unable to get a seller to give you seller financing you will still be happy to buy the property with cash because you are getting such a deep discount on the price. If you can get a property under contract that is a fantastic deal you should be able to raise the capital to buy it. There are always investors around who are waiting for the "deal of the century". Make your cash offer equivalent to the "deal of the century."

Offer #2 is a small amount of seller financing

This offer usually shows only 20-40% of the purchase price as seller financing. The balance of the price can be cash (hopefully someone else's) or a traditional loan from a bank. This option is on the spreadsheet to show the seller how a little *more money* can be made on the property over time if they offer a little bit of seller financing.

This offer can be a higher purchase price than the cash offer. The sums of the payments you will make to the seller are outlined. The spreadsheet adds up those payments and shows the seller how beneficial seller financing can be compared to cash. It makes it very clear that the seller gets the price plus interest on the money being financed.

Make sure the seller understands that if you do end up holding the property *long-term* you will refinance and pay off the loan. Typically you will ask for 1 to 2 years of seller financing with the balance due at the end of that time. (Again, this assumes you are changing the property to a "Higher and Better Use") Whether you sell the property or refinance it, the seller will get their full amount within that time.

The only time you would do long-term financing is if *long-term income is crucial to the seller.* (Or if you are buying a property for existing cash flow that does not have an "upside" or way to improve its value) If long term income is crucial to the seller make sure you get a low (market or lower) fixed interest rate to cover your loan if you end up keeping the project long-term. Remember that initially you can use an adjustable rate to lower your expenses if there is an occupancy issue.

Offer #3 shows a large amount of seller financing.

This offer will normally show seller financing of 75-100% of the price. I suggest you offer the highest price to the seller on this offer because it is the easiest and least expensive type of purchase for you. There are no loan costs, no lender points, no appraisal, loan paperwork, red tape, qualifying etc.

One of the fantastic outcomes you will get from using this spreadsheet is that it will open up the conversation about seller financing. If the sellers only have 25% equity they might say, "I can't finance that much." (Unless they understand about how to wrap a loan) When this is said, it's your opportunity to have a longer discussion with them about their equity and just what it can do for them.

The interest rates stated on the example are just suggestions. You should play around with them and see what works for you on a deal-by-deal basis. The monthly payments are also just a suggestion. Some investors offer to pay quarterly or yearly or even less frequently. (As you know from our "Top 23 Terms to negotiate" chapter) In addition you may wish to pay principal and interest. (Instead of interest only as shown) This option will trigger the seller's capital gains tax though, so why make your payment higher?

Offer #4 is the offer to partner with the seller.

Always offer to partner with sellers when you put together your "4-offer spreadsheet". (This is true mainly when you are buying a property where you are going to change the use to a "Higher and Better Use" It may not be necessary if you are buying multi-family properties for a long term hold.) You do this to see if you can do the deal without having to *pay for* the property up front *or* pay for the changes out of your pocket.

Yes, you read that right. If sellers choose to partner with you then you will ask them to put the property in your name while you execute the "Change of Use". If they want to get a maximum return then you also ask them to pay for *all of the changes*. When you sell or refinance you will pay them the full price for their property, return the money they paid for the changes *and* give them a portion of the profits.

Remember, the other reason to always offer to partner with a seller is to help protect you later. Always mention in your final agreed-upon contract that you offered to partner with the sellers and were *refused* so that they could receive their money sooner. That way when you sell the property again in the future, a seller cannot come back to you and say you should have paid more money for the property. This doesn't typically happen when you are upfront with the seller all along, but it is nice to be covered just in case.

On the next page is an example of a "4-offer spreadsheet". The first column shows an item of the contract, the second shows the terms of the 1st offer, and the third shows the terms of the 2nd offer. The 3rd and 4th offers are on the next page.

Numbers tell a story. Spend some time studying the numbers so you can understand the reasoning and intent of each offer. Take special notice that this spreadsheet clearly shows the seller how much *extra* will be made by seller financing!

Sample "4-Offer Spreadsheet": Offers 1&2

Contract Element	#1 Cash Purchase	#2 20% Owner Seller Finance
Total Price	$200,000	$225,000
Cash Down Payment or 1st lien	$200,000	$180,000 Bank 1st lien
Financing	n/a	$45,000 Seller 2nd lien
Seller Finance Monthly Income	n/a	7% interest only payments Full payoff within 24 months Monthly Interest = $262.50
Total Interest		2 Years Total Interest = $6,300
Cash to Seller at Closing	$200,000	$180,000
Payback at call time		$45,000
Gross Profit to seller	**$200,000**	**(Price+Interest) $231,300**
Timing of Profits to Seller	At closing	Within 24 months
Earnest Money	$3,000	$3,000
Closing Date	7 days after due diligence	7 days after due diligence
Feasibility Period	45 days	45 days
Vital Clauses	Seller Rejected Partnership Buyer's partner to approve	Seller Rejected Partnership Buyer's partner to approve

Sample "4-Offer Spreadsheet": Offers 3&4

Contract Element	#3 90% Owner Seller Financed 1st Lien	#4 Seller Partnership
Total Price	$250,000	$250,000*
Cash Down Payment	$25,000	n/a
Financing / Terms	$225,000 Seller 1st lien	n/a
	8% interest only payments	n/a
	Full payoff within 36 months	n/a
Seller Finance Income	Monthly Interest = $1,500	
Total Interest	$54,000	n/a
Cash to Seller at Closing	$25,000	n/a
Cash at balloon	$225,000	
Gross Profit to seller	**(Price+Interest) $304,000**	**Unknown**
Timing of Total to Seller	Within 36 months	Within 24 months
Earnest Money	$3,000	$0
Closing Date	7 days after due diligence	n/a
Option Period	45 days	30 days
Special Provisions	Seller Rejected Partnership Buyer's partner to approve	* Paid to seller when re-sold or refinanced. Will also be paid back all "cost to change" plus a 40% split of profits.

FREE Online Resources

I have decided to offer this form for *free* in a spreadsheet format you can modify to fit your own needs. Just go to **www.mikewatsoninvesting.com/sfbook** and click on the "4-offer Spreadsheet" Here you will find a blank spreadsheet. Save it to your computer and plug in your numbers on your offers and go buy some properties!

Once you set up your offers the most important thing to do is to *talk with the sellers*. Show them how the spreadsheet works and show them the *higher* proceeds with seller financing. Show them how they will get passive income from their equity. You might even compare their income to what they would get if they put their *after tax* proceeds in a money market account. That one discussion has created many seller financers!

Often, this is what will happen. If the sellers have any interest in getting cash flow they will start to talk to you about the interest rate you have offered. Be willing to be flexible with the rate. Doing seller financing will save you so much in the way of loan fees that you can pay 2-3% more on your interest rate and still do better than if you had to get a loan from a bank. Once they are thinking positively about offering the financing, you are on your way to creating a win/win deal. This spreadsheet is fantastic for helping to build rapport with sellers. When you build enough rapport you will get the sellers to tell you their real needs.

The key is to determine which of the seller's needs are the most critical. There may only be one, but there may be two or three. I have never had a seller who had more than three *critical* needs. Here are some of the most common seller's needs:

1. Must get asking price.
2. Must close on a certain day.
3. Must avoid foreclosure
4. Must get rid of property management.
5. Must get a certain amount of income.
6. Must get income for a certain amount of time. (May be combined with #5)
7. Income must start at a certain time. (Common when retirement is a few years away)
8. Must get rid of paying the loan. (Similar to #3 but may not be in trouble of foreclosure)
9. Must feel like they are getting a fair deal.

If you are able to pinpoint which needs are the most critical for the sellers then you can structure the offer to meet their needs. At this point they will usually give you any of the other terms you want to include. Why? They will do this for you because you will have *met their needs*. Remember most sellers only have two or three real needs. If you find out what these needs are, meet them, and then create terms around them that make the deal work for you, why wouldn't they agree? The truth is, they will.

Remember the time I gave the seller the $1 down payment for earnest money? He allowed me to do this because I agreed to solve his *number one* problem. I got him out from under a mortgage on a duplex where he had no income. Sellers really don't care about the rest of the terms if you meet their most *critical* ones. Use the "4-offer spreadsheet" to start digging to find out what your seller's needs are, then use the "Top 23 Terms to Negotiate with Seller Financing" to create a win/win deal for you both.

The "4-offer spreadsheet" is the fastest way to expose a seller's needs.

~Mike Watson

DE-COLLATERALIZATION OR... RAISING CAPITAL THE FUN WAY

DE-COLLATERALIZATION OR... RAISING CAPITAL THE FUN WAY

Now that you have a pretty good grasp on seller financing and how to explain it to a seller I'd like to move on to a technique I call "*de*-collateralization". Don't let the big word trip you up. All it means is that you are separating the property from the loan. In other words you are "removing the collateral" for the loan.

You might wonder what this has to do with seller financing. Let me explain. When you get a loan for a property from a bank or mortgage company they would never allow you to remove the collateral from your loan. That would be so risky for them that they would never do it. On the other hand, if you pay your payments to a seller on time or even early for a few months or years there might be an incentive for a seller to allow you to remove the property as collateral for the loan.

Why would you want to do that? Well, here is the best reason. You would want to remove the property from the loan in order to *raise capital*. When you separate the loan from the property all you have to do is have the lien holder release the lien from the Deed of Trust. Typically this happens when you sell the property and pay off the loan.

But think about what would happen if you sold or re-financed the property and did *not* have to pay off the loan. You would get all of the proceeds in cash and could use that cash to buy another property. You would still owe the old seller their payments and the principal, now in the form of a promissory note with *no collateral*, but you would be able to use the cash. You could use it to enhance the property, buy another property or even make your payments. (Do NOT spend this on frivolous non-income or profit producing items!)

This is a very advanced technique even though it is quite simple. Most people take a little time to completely understand it. I have several students who have used it successfully. Let me give you an example.

Remember when Julie met with the seller and showed him her "4-offer spreadsheet"? Remember how the seller was so excited about giving her seller financing because he wanted to have income without property management? How do you think that seller felt when Julie called him eight months later and said, "I have a contract to sell the property and now I am going to pay off your loan."?

Obviously this was not what the seller wanted. Julie had done such a good job of teaching him the merits of seller financing that he wanted to have several years of passive income from that loan he had given her. He did not want his cash back. He didn't want to pay the taxes on his gain or lose his monthly cash flow. He was not happy with Julie's new offer. Let's see what happened next.

Julie called the seller about a week before she sold the property. She told him she was selling the property and was planning to pay off the loan. There was silence on the other line. Finally, he told her that he really did not want his equity back. He wanted to keep getting payments. So, after some thought Julie said, "Here are some options. I can pay your loan off. I can move your loan to another deal I am doing. Or I can just remove your loan from the property and keep paying you. If you chose that option I will increase your interest rate a little to help you with the risk."

I know you are thinking Julie was crazy to even ask the seller this, but remember the seller wanted *income*. He was sold on the idea and not looking forward to getting 2.5% from a bank compared to 9% from Julie. The seller said, "Let me sleep on it and I'll give you an answer in the morning."

The next morning Julie's phone rang. When she picked it up the seller said, "I want to do number three. I only have one question. What happens if you don't pay me?"

She explained her circumstances with her other properties and what she was going to do with the money (buy an income producing apartment complex that would pay his payments) and he was satisfied. Three weeks later Julie sold the property and the old seller released the lien from the property without asking Julie to pay it off. That meant Julie received all of the cash at the closing.

Instead of a deed of trust and a note on the property she now only has a promissory note with the seller. She increased her interest rate on the loan (so he got paid more) and also extended the balloon for several more years (so she had the option to pay it off further in the future). She then used the monies from the closing to buy another property which she then changed to its "Highest and Best" use (increased density, increased rents and lowered expenses). At some point Julie will pay off his loan (probably when she sells the apartments) but for now it is an amazing way to tap into capital for more deals.

If you are going to try this technique it is smart to make sure you have equity in a property that you can refinance. That way when the loan is due you can sell or refinance in order to get the loan paid. In addition, with the funds you receive, it is a good idea to buy a property with cash flow. That way those funds can make the payments for the loan rather than any payments having to come directly out of your pocket.

If this seems like a stretch, read the section over. I have students in my classes who frequently use this technique. It is one of the best ways to raise capital for deals! Just think, the property was financed by the seller and then that seller also financed your *next* property. There is money for deals everywhere if you just know how to find it.

> " When you de-collateralize a loan you will feel the true power of how to use seller financing for raising capital.
>
> **~Mike Watson** "

DO NOT FORGET THESE 5 VITAL TECHNIQUES!

CHAPTER **19**

DO NOT FORGET THESE 5 VITAL TECHNIQUES!

We have made huge leaps as far as learning how to use these incredible seller financing techniques. We have discussed the basics of seller financing, how to negotiate a fantastic contract, how to create "Green Mortgages" and many other concepts. I now want to take a step back and go over a few of the details that must be covered in order to implement some of these ideas. These concepts are crucial for ensuring you don't get into a sticky situation.

1. Partial Re-conveyance

I'd like to tell you about an investor who came to my classes just a little bit too late. This person had recently purchased an apartment building. When he got his loan on the property he didn't tell the bank that he was planning on doing a condominium conversion to the complex.

This gentleman closed on the apartment complex and then spent a whole lot of money refurbishing the units. During this time he even *evicted* paying tenants so he could remodel and sell units as condominiums.

One day a buyer came in and made him an acceptable offer for one of the units. This investor was going to make a decent profit so he accepted the offer. Then the buyer went to a bank to get a loan. In the process the title company pulled the title policy and it showed the loan on the apartment complex.

When the title company asked the bank for the payoff for that *one unit* the bank was confused and said "What are you talking about?" The title company stated that the owner was selling one of the units and therefore they needed to know how much of the loan needed to be paid off in order to release the lien on that unit.

Unfortunately the bank said, "We are not set up to do a *partial re-conveyance*." This meant the bank never agreed to split up its loan into smaller pieces (that is, allow it to be paid off one unit at a time). It was not aware the owner of the apartment complex would want this done so this was not put into the loan documents.

> **Partial Re-conveyance** – When a lien holder agrees to release the lien from a portion of a property when a designated part of the lien is paid off.
>
> Definition

As you might imagine this wreaked havoc on the deal. It completely stopped the seller from being able to sell the *individual* units. Therefore until the seller refinanced into a loan that he was able to split up and pay off in small portions or, he paid the whole loan off with his own or private cash, he was unable to complete his condo-conversion and make *any* profits.

In addition, the buyer was very upset. He wanted to purchase a unit and move in immediately and now it wasn't known if the property could even be bought.

I don't know if this seller ever sold his property. Unfortunately he didn't stay in my courses long enough to create from innovative solutions. My guess is he either had to end up renting the units or hopefully he found a bank that would refinance his loan and partially re-convey each unit when a portion of the loan was paid off.

This example demonstrates how important it is to know the ins and outs of all types of financing. But how does this relate to seller financing? If you are buying a property and intend to split it up in any way (where there will be more than one owner) and you get financing from the *seller or any other party* at all you *must* negotiate the partial re-conveyance terms up front.

In other words, the decision must be made between yourself and all lien holders as to how much must be paid off in order for them to release any portion of the property from the loan. That way you can sell the individual pieces separately without any cloud on the title.

Cloud on Title – Any item on a title that represents a lien or encumbrance.

Definition

Here is an example of a partial re-conveyance. Imagine you buy a 4-plex and do a condo-conversion. Let's say you paid $400,000 for the 4-plex and the seller gave you $100,000 seller financing. Now you are ready to sell the first unit (A) for $150,000. The buyer gets a new loan for $150,000. When unit A closes, you pay $100,000 to the original seller who then releases the whole original loan from that *one* unit. He also lowers $100,000 from your original $400,000. Then you only have a $300,000 loan left on the remaining 3 units

Here is how this would look:

- 4-plex loan of $400,000
- Pay-off 1 unit, remaining loan of $300,000
- Pay-off another unit, remaining loan of $200,000

PARTIAL RE-CONVEYANCE EXAMPLE

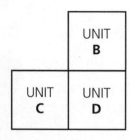

· 4-plex loan of $400k

· Unit A sells, Pay off $100k of $400k.
· Seller releases Unit A.
· $300k loan left over.

· Unit B sells, Pay off $100k of $300k.
· Seller releases Unit B.
· $200k loan left over.

Each time you sell a unit you receive profits (or cash flow if you seller finance your equity) and your loan with the original seller goes down.

2. Splintering

Another tool I teach investors is called "splintering". This technique is very useful when you intend to create more owners (increase density by increasing tax ID numbers). It allows you to *pass on* to the next buyers any benefits of seller financing you received when you purchased the property.

As an example lets assume you buy a lot that is large enough to subdivide into 4 lots. When you buy the lot the seller is kind enough (or smart enough) to offer you seller financing. That is because you explained the benefits so well when you first made your offer.

After you do the subdivision and have a buyer for your first lot it might be smart to go back to the owner and have another discussion about splintering the loan. (Remember you would have already negotiated the partial re-conveyance part of the loan. Splintering is an *additional* useful tool.) When you go to the seller you could ask to splinter the loan which means that you would be allowed to split the original loan up into four pieces.

But how would this benefit you as the new seller? (Especially if you already have the partial re-conveyance.) As an example, let's say you negotiated with the seller to have a "Green Mortgage" loan or an assumable loan. Now you would have *four* assumable loans! When you sell each of the four lots you could *pass on* the seller financing you received to each new buyer. Then you could either take your profits or offer the buyer a second lien as seller financing from you. This buyer would then pay the original owner the first lien payment and pay you the second lien payment. In this scenario *no new loan* with a bank or mortgage company needs to be processed at all!

Here, just like in our partial re-conveyance example you have a $400,000 original loan. You already have the partial re-conveyance and now we will show the original seller allowing us to splinter the loan so they can keep the income. When you get your buyer for the first lot you can call the owner and ask if the new buyer could assume 25% of the original loan.

Here is how that looks.

- Original loan with the one lot $100,000
- Four $25,000 loans to each new buyer.

SPLINTERING EXAMPLE 1

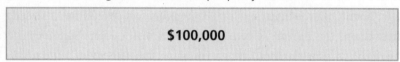

Original loan when property is one lot

$100,000

Four **$25k** assumable loans when four lots

$25k $25k $25k $25k

If you are working with sellers who understand the incredible benefits seller financing has to offer they may be willing to offer this as an option from the very first day you buy the property. If they aren't as savvy, they may need to see that their income from the seller financing will stop if they don't allow the loan to be assumed and splintered.

This is one of the most advanced techniques I teach and it is also one of the most valuable. Imagine how much you can ask for a property if you can offer *all* of the financing to the buyer. You will have increased *two* of the five densities (number of owners and terms). You will increase your profits, your equity positions, and your income from notes receivables.

In addition the original sellers will continue to get their desired cash flows. If they are leery of this technique you may want to offer them a higher interest rate or a point at the second closing to give them an incentive to make the deal work for all parties. Most of the time I haven't needed to offer them anything better than their original terms because they are in a better situation with four first mortgages than with only one. Let me show you why this is true.

Consider that you purchased a lot for $100,000 and the seller gave you 100% seller financing. Now the seller has a $100,000 mortgage on a property worth $100,000. The seller's collateral (the property) is *equal* to the indebtedness (their loan). This is not a great position to be in because if values fall and the seller has to take the property back then they may not get their money when they re-sell the property.

On the other hand, if you split the property and are allowed to split the loan into four pieces, each loan would then be for $25,000. However the lots are now worth more than one quarter of the original price. Let's say you could now sell the lots for $50,000 each. This would mean that the seller has four $25,000 first liens on four properties worth $50,000 each. That means there is *$25,000* in equity behind each loan. (Instead of *none!*)

The original seller therefore has a much better loan-to-value ratio with a splintered loan than with one loan. If the seller had to take all four lots back the market would have had to crash down 50% before they even touched their original profits. Typically it is easy to get a seller to agree to this once the principle is understood because the loans will be more secure.

SPLINTERING EXAMPLE 2

Seller's benefit

One lot's value = $100k and loan value = $100k

$100k

$25k   **$25k**   **$25k**   **$25k**

The Four Lot value = **$200k**, but four loan value = **$100k**,
Therefore splintering has created four safer loans!

= Equity behind the loan

Another way to handle splintering is to get the seller to give you several loans at the *original closing*. Make sure that the number of loans you are given equals the number of properties you will end up with at the end of your conversion. Also make sure the amounts of the loans are proportional to the future values of the individually divided lots or units.

Let's see how this would work using the same example as above. You would buy the property and get *four* $25,000 mortgages for your $100,000 purchase instead of *one* $100,000 mortgage. This would start the splintering process at the beginning of the transaction instead of waiting until you are partially completed.

If the seller is open-minded it is better to have a discussion up front about splintering but not as vital as getting the partial re-conveyance approved prior to closing. That is because the splintering just allows you to give those loans to the next buyer but the partial re-conveyance would stop you from being able to sell.

There is one other advantage to the seller if splitting the loan is agreed to at the original closing. Now, one or more of the notes can be sold separately. Here is how that would work.

Note selling

One of the ways that sellers can offer seller financing and still receive cash at closing or shortly thereafter, is through selling their note receivable. One of the most prized notes for note buyers to purchase is a real estate note collateralized by a great asset.

If a seller had four $25,000 note receivables one could be sold to a note broker at a slight discount for cash and the others could be kept for cash flow. This allows the buyer to get 100% seller financing at closing and the seller to get a lump sum of cash right after closing plus payments over time on the other three notes.

This technique allows sellers to choose when they want the

cash. If they choose to do so, the note need not be sold immediately. Getting four $25,000 notes also works well in this case because the seller can sell different notes at different times to get lump sums of cash when it is needed regardless of the call or term of the loan. You can be very creative with this technique.

All in all, purchasing properties with multiple Trust Deed and Notes (also known as "splintering" at the original closure) gives a lot more flexibility, creativity and options for profit for both the buyer and seller in a transaction.

3. Subordination

One seller financing technique I discuss is when a buyer gets a first lien from a bank or mortgage company and then the seller offers the buyer a second lien for their equity. In this way a buyer could purchase a property without having to put very much or possibly even no money as a down payment.

There are always a lot of questions when I talk about this at my events. Many people think banks will not let a buyer do this. They think the bank who is giving the first lien will require a down payment.

There are two things to consider here in order to make this technique work. The first is that usually a bank or mortgage company will want buyers to have some of their own cash in the deal. The difference is when you as a buyer are going to be adding a lot of value to a property very quickly after closing.

The whole basis of "The Foundation to Success" is the "Highest and Best" use. You add value to a property by increasing its density. Remember our talk about the five types of density? (Number of units, amount of square footage, number of tax ID numbers or owners, income, and terms) If you are going to add value to the property very quickly after closing, many times smaller local banks *will* allow you to appraise the property at the higher value. When you do this then they will allow you to come to closing with little or no funds.

The second thing you have to remember is that the bank or mortgage company that gives you the first lien will require the seller financing part of the purchase to be a 2nd lien. That means they will require the sellers to sign paperwork stating that their lien is subordinate to (or behind) the bank's loan. If you do not discuss this with the sellers when negotiating your offer, they may be very unhappy at the closing.

The reason they may be unhappy is that when they sign the subordination clause they are stating that someone else will be taking a first position in front of them. This means that if there is a foreclosure, they get paid second after the first lien holder is paid in full.

Many times the first lien will be a construction or development loan, especially if you are buying a property you are going to improve. If this is the case make sure the sellers know you will only be drawing funds from that loan as you make improvements. That way they will feel more comfortable about being in second position because the collateral for their loan will be worth *more* money.

Many times when you explain all of these things to sellers they will trust you and be more willing to offer seller financing. They will understand you are taking care of them as well as yourself in the transaction. You may find that when you develop their trust you will have raised capital to help finance your deals for many years to come.

4. Cross-collateralization (Also called re-collateralization)

We have already discussed De-Collaterlization - where you remove the collateral from the loan. Here is another related technique you can use to raise capital.

The term cross-collateralization literally means that you are going to *change* the collateral of a loan. In other words you will have the same loan but you will move it from one property to another.

This is an important idea to discuss with sellers who are offering you financing. This discussion will show sellers you are an active investor and will always be looking into other deals. Wouldn't it be nice to be able to move a loan from one property to another and take the full sales price from the first deal and use it for another purchase?

To discuss this with sellers you should show them how they will receive cash flows and not have to own property. Then you can clearly explain to them that when you either sell or refinance the property, the title company will make you pay the seller's loan off. Unfortunately, that means those precious monthly income checks will promptly come to a screeching halt.

One way to avoid this painful experience is to have a cross-collateralization clause in the loan which says you may move a loan from one property to another. That way when the time comes to pay off the sellers' loan, you can move the loan to another property and keep making their payment. Always let them know they will never have a higher loan-to-value ratio than they do now. They will always have the current amount or more equity behind their loan. (And make sure they do) This should help them feel better about the clause.

If they are still reluctant, you can offer the same incentives we discussed before, extend the length of the loan, increase interest rate, pay a point etc.

The benefit to you as the buyer is you can move the loan to another deal and then have access to much more cash when you sell or refinance to do other deals. This is another example of how seller financing is a way of raising capital!

As an example let's assume you buy a home that cost you $200,000 and the sellers did 100% seller financing with you. After you change the use of the property and increase it's value then you sell it for $300,000. At that time instead of paying the sellers their $200,000 they allow you to move that loan to a different property you own.

If you own a 4-plex that is worth $800,000 and you currently have a $300,000 loan on it you could add the $200,000 from the home as a 2nd lien. That way the sellers would have equity behind their loan.

Next you could take the full $300,000 of proceeds from the sale of the home and go buy another property. In this visual example we have you buy a $400,000 duplex. In this manner you can create incredible leverage to buy more properties with *one* seller. Notice that instead of just the $100,000 of equity you would have received at closing when you sold the home you now have another property worth much more.

CROSS-COLLATERALIZATION EXAMPLE

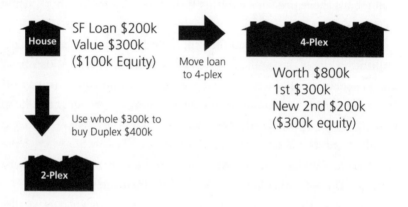

Why might you want to move the loan even if you don't sell the original home? What if you wanted to build an 8 unit apartment complex and you wanted to get a big construction loan. It would be much easier to attain that loan if the property you own is free and clear. One way to have the property be free and clear is to move the loan to a different property. (In this case the 4-plex) Keep this technique in mind whenever you want to raise capital.

5. Novation Agreement

Let's assume you bought a property and the seller agreed to finance it to you and let the loan be assumable. (It's "green"!) You are now in a great position to offer this property as an assumable loan to other buyers.

However, what happens when a new buyer enters the picture and assumes this financing? Are you still responsible for that loan? If the new buyer defaults on the loan, is the original seller legally allowed to come back to you for the payments?

The answer is "yes" there is an implied liability, especially if you do not cover yourself properly. Just how can you protect yourself? First, always have a good attorney draw up your seller financing documents. Wording must be put in the loan documents that lays out the fact that all liability will switch to the next buyer.

Furthermore, I always get extra coverage by including a "Novation" agreement. A Novation agreement is a document that explicitly states that the old seller cannot come to you if the loan is assumed by a new buyer. It says that the old seller releases you from all liability of the loan when the loan is assumed by a new buyer.

If you discuss this with the seller during negotiations and get it in *writing* that a novation agreement will be signed at the time of assumption, your coverage will be much greater.

The main lesson for you in all these examples is the importance of talking with professionals about your entire deal. You need to talk with your real estate broker, accountant, attorney, lender, a title company and possibly even your city, prior to signing a deal where a lot of money could potentially be lost. Improper documentation could cause serious problems for you as well as for other people.

My book "The Highest and Best Real Estate Investment" has many tips like these for making sure your deals work. It even has a very long chapter that goes into how to evaluate your deal completely before its feasibility time frame ends. I highly suggest you read that book before you do any deals. It is well worth the time and effort to learn from my (and my students') mistakes and lessons rather than blindly going through the entire process. You do not need to reinvent the wheel. Let me help you through every step of the way.

CHAPTER 20

MY "SECRET" GOAL

MY "SECRET" GOAL

have to admit, I have more than one goal in this book. The first and most obvious goal is to teach you the most powerful tool you can have in your toolbox for investing in real estate, which is *seller financing*. My "secret" goal however, is to change how you think about wealth.

Wealth is usually thought of as cash in your pocket. In truth, wealth has a much more expanded definition. It includes such things as having cash on hand from profits, cash flow from income properties, equity positions and cash flow from notes receivable. If you are able to incorporate all of these different types of wealth into your investing then you are creating a much stronger type of wealth with a wider and deeper foundation. This is exactly why I teach "The Foundation to Success".

One major habit in our society that stands in the way of our wealth is how we spend our money. Most people spend what they earn and just a little bit *more*. Individuals are in debt at record levels. Bankruptcies, which are nothing more than a person stating, "I can't handle the debt I have created for myself", are also at record levels. The main cause of this is our perspective on wealth.

We need to learn how to create "Wealth with Legs." This is money, but it is also profits or cash flow that keeps coming in the door when we are working and when we are *not* working. When we do a deal that creates a big profit, we can spend it all very easily. However, when we create a profit that comes in the form of many payments over time, it is much more difficult to spend all of that profit.

Investors have traditionally been profit driven. We need a new breed of investors who are driven by cash flow. Cash flow comes in two forms. It comes in the form of net positive cash flows from income producing properties and *notes receivable* from issuing seller financing. How different would your life be if your wealth came to you in the form of many monthly payments you receive over very long periods of time?

This is why seller financing is so crucial at this point in our history. Property values are down and property income is up. In the past, the value of income properties has followed the strength of their income. That is how they are evaluated and why they are bought. We are currently seeing income producing properties in major metropolitan markets that are selling retail for half or less of what they were two to three years ago. The crazy part is that they have better occupancy rates and *higher* rents than they used to!

Additionally, since sellers are having such a hard time financially, many are not only considering seller financing, they are begging for it. You hold in your hands the key to becoming a master of this great art right now! My deepest wish is for you to take this knowledge and create wealth for yourself and your family for generations to come. We will all look back at this market in a few years wondering why we didn't buy everything we possibly could. It is time that we as investors start to think differently. The potential is too incredible to ignore.

So remember, the only way to be truly wealthy is to redefine wealth. Wealth is actually a combination of four things: *cash on hand, cash flow from income properties, equity positions and cash flow from notes receivable.*

When you shift your thinking to include these methods of earning money, your definition of wealth will shift to the more profitable long term way of earning a living. I want to end this book with a technique that has the ability to bring you three if not all four of these types of profits in just *one* deal.

I suggest you read this book over and over and also attend one of my Advanced Seller Financing Degree Camps. This will enable you to feel at ease and confident about seller financing. Seller financing can and will change the investing world. Be a part of this revolution.

I invite you to learn how to *buy and sell properties without using a bank* and become wealthy with all of the rest of us who are learning and practicing these techniques!

> True wealth is much more than just cash. True wealth includes cash on hand, cash flow from income properties, equity positions and cash flow from notes receivable!
>
> **~Mike Watson**

THE "ONE HIT WONDER" OR... PROPERTY-LESS PASSIVE INCOME FOR LIFE

THE "ONE HIT WONDER" OR... PROPERTY-LESS PASSIVE INCOME FOR LIFE

I have a technique that is so incredibly exciting I can hardly contain myself when talking about it. It is a program that can literally change your life for a very long time with just *one* deal. I call it the "One Hit Wonder".

I teach this technique in my classes as part of a program within the "Foundation to Success". The "Foundation to Success" teaches you how to find a property and make it worth more by doing something to it. Usually that "something" is changing the "use" of the property and it always involves increasing one of the five types of density.

In order to keep demonstrate this program I want to go through an example. Let's say you purchase a 10 unit apartment complex and then do a condominium conversion on the units. The conversion makes the property worth more because you are increasing the number of owners. (One of our forms of density) It went from one owner, you, to 10 owners as each unit is sold separately.

Here is how the numbers could look.

The Deal:

Purchase Price	$1,250,000
Costs for Conversion	$150,000
Carrying Costs of Loans	
minus rents (Property/Construction)	$50,000
Closing Costs when you sell	$150,000
Total Cost of entire project	$1,600,000

Divide that total by 10 units
which gives you a complete per-unit cost of $160,000

We assume during your deal evaluation, you determined (conservatively) that the newly remodeled condo units will each sell for $250,000. When you sell the units this is how you determine your profit on each unit.

With a sales price of	$250,000
Complete costs per unit	- $160,000
Net proceeds (or net equity position) per unit	$90,000

Keep this *$90,000 worth of net profit per unit* in mind as I go through the next five scenarios. In each case this $90,000 *per unit* is what we are calculating, the *net profit* of the deal. We are going yo manipulate the manner in which you receive those profits and thereby manipulate the total amount you will receive. I am going to walk through this deal using five different scenarios. That way I will demonstrate the many ways you can make different kinds of profits within just one deal.

Option #1
(Sell the units and get cash at closing)

If you sell all of the units for *cash to you at closing* your total profit will be $900,000! ($90,000 x 10 units) Your net worth would go up by this amount minus the taxes owed. (Probably around $600,000 increase in net worth)

This would be considered the traditional way of investing. First you put your money into the deal and then you work on the property to make it more valuable and finally get your returns in cash at closing. So far this looks like an incredible deal! But let's see what *else* you could do with your equity.

Option #2
(Keep the property and
have an increased net worth)

Just by owning the property you have increased your net worth by $1,050,000. Why is this number more than the $900,000 of cash proceeds at closing? Because you won't have closing costs of $150,000 if you *keep* the property. Now that you have created this equity you could refinance the property, pay off all of your loans and keep the property with the equity. This increase in your net worth is the second function of wealth in the system I teach.

Option #3
(Keep the property as a rental for income)

The third type of wealth is to have income from a cash flowing property. In this specific case you may not have even done the condo conversion. Hopefully the property you purchased was already cash flowing as it stood. If not there are several other methods I teach for increasing income on a rental property. One of which is to implement a tenant reimbursement program for all utilities. (There are dozens of other ideas I talk about in my "The Highest and Best Real Estate Investment" book.)

You could also remodel and refinance the property and then increase rents based on an upgraded property.

But keep reading, I have another technique that will show you a much better way to accomplish an increased cash flow! If you structure this deal correctly you will be able to offer some incredible terms to the buyers of the individual condos *and* take advantage of the full seller financing benefits for *yourself!*

Option #4 (Seller finance for cash flow)

What if you sell the units and offer seller financing? This is how you build an income stream from creating notes payable. Here is one way it could work.

Let's say that instead of selling all of the units for cash or keeping the property as a rental, you decide to seller finance a portion of your equity to each buyer. In this example you give them each a loan for 20% of the purchase price and they will pay you *interest only* payments of 10% for 10 years on that loan. (These are very reasonable 2nd lien terms.)

The buyers will go get their own 80% first mortgage from a bank or lender on their $250,000 purchase price. That first loan amount will be $200,000. ($250,000 x 80%) Their second loan amount will be $50,000 with you. ($250,000 x 20%) The first thing you might notice is that the buyers are now paying ZERO DOWN. Think your units might sell quickly with those terms?

Here is how it plays out for *each unit:*

The new buyer's loan of (80% of $250,000) $200,000
Complete cost of each unit...- $160,000
Equals at closing to you..*$40,000 cash*
plus a $50,000 note to you!

*Notice that the $40,000 and $50,000 totals our original net profit per unit of $90,000.

If you sold all 10 units and gave the buyers these seller finance terms you would end up with a total of $400,000 in cash at closing. ($40,000 x 10 units) The best part is you would also have $500,000 in notes receivable (10 units x $50,000 per unit).

Since the 10 new owners are paying you 10% *interest only* payments on those notes you will receive $50,000 *per year* in *interest* which totals $4,166 per month! (With no maintenance or management) Ideally this will last for the full ten years until your loan has its balloon and then those owners will still owe you the *principal balance* of the 10 notes.

Imagine what it would be like to do *one project* and walk out with $400,000 cash in hand and $50,000 in interest income per year for ten years PLUS $500,000 in principal paid to you when the notes come due in ten years.

At the end of ten years when all of the interest is paid and the principal is paid back here is what you would have in *total profit* on that one deal:

Total Cash at closings...$400,000
Interest paid out to you *over* ten years $500,000
Principal due to you *in* ten years $500,000
Total Profit...$1,400,000

*Please note that in this scenario you are only financing a *portion* of your profits. You *never* want to finance any of your hard costs. (The

$160,000) This is the key to safer seller financing.

I also want you to notice that in this example you have increased your profits on this one deal by half a million dollars just by offering terms to the buyers. This is a perfect example of how seller financing can increase the value of a deal much more than if you just sell your project outright in a traditional way. I hope the benefits of offering seller financing are becoming clearer to you. In this next option look at how the numbers differ with a small change in the seller financing terms.

Option #5
(More seller financing for more cash flow)

If you had instead decided to offer the buyers seller financing on 30% of the purchase price instead of 20% the numbers would change to look like this on each unit:

Their bank loan of (70% of $250,000).......................................$175,000
Complete cost of each unit...- $160,000
Equals at closing to you...*$15,000 cash*
plus a $75,000 note to you.

*Note that the $15,000 and $75,000 totals our original net profit of $90,000 per unit.

In this scenario if you sold all 10 units with these terms you would end up with a total of $150,000 in cash at closing, ($15,000 x 10 units) and the best part is you would also have $750,000 in notes receivable (10 units x $75,000 per unit). Since the 10 new owners are all paying you 10% interest only payments on those notes you will receive *$75,000 per year* in interest or *$6,250 per month* in property-less passive income! Ideally this will last for the full ten years until your loan has its balloon and then those owners will pay you the principal balance of the notes.

At the end of the ten years when all the interest has been paid and the notes are paid back you would have on this one deal a *total profit* of:

Total Cash at closings $150,000
Interest paid out to you *over* ten years $750,000
Principal due to you *in* ten years $750,000
Total Profit $1,650,000

Let's compare the different profits from each scenario:

In option #1 you had a cash profit of $900,000. This was the net profit per door of $90,000 times 10 units. In option #2 you had a net worth increase of $1,050,000. We did not calculate the profits of option #3 but they would be the net rental income of how many years you own the property plus whatever profits you make when you sell. (There are too many factors to calculate this long term option)

In option #4 which was 20% seller financing the total profit increases to $1,400,000. This is an extra $500,000 to you for *helping people* obtain housing. If you had decided to go with option #5 and seller finance 30% of the purchase price to buyers then your profits would have increased even more to $1,650,000. By using seller financing you can take a great deal and make it unbelievable!

To make you think one step further, imagine this: All of these options assume you either keep all ten units as rentals or sell all ten units. What would happen if you sell three of the units for cash, sell three with seller financing and hold four of them as rental units? All in *one deal* you would have equity, cash in hand, cash flow from income property and cash flow from promissory notes to you!

Imagine how different your life would be if you offered seller financing and had, as a result, one of the outcomes previously outlined. Just to expand your thinking one more time, imagine if you did just one deal a year like this for five years. You could easily be making $350,000 per year from notes receivable alone! Seller financing *can and will* change your life when you take the leap of faith.

Passive Income for Life

Now that you understand how a "One Hit Wonder" works I want to present another idea to take you a couple of steps further. The most common feedback I get with the "One Hit Wonder" program is "Wow that is incredible! I love the thought of doubling my profits and getting that income for several years."

The second most common feedback I get is, "I want to have income from my properties for *life* so I'm not going to sell at all. I'm going to hold the property for rental income." That thought is a valid one and is even one of the options I suggest you explore further. But keep reading.

What if I could show you a way to turn the "One Hit Wonder" *into income for life*? Let's look closer at some of the terms you could use and how to manipulate them to reach your desired outcome. What would happen if, when you made the 20% or 30% seller financed loans, some additional provisions were added to the terms of these notes?

For instance, a "pre-payment penalty" could be added. (This means a fee must be paid to you if the principal balance of the loan is paid off prior to the call or balloon date) The penalty is meant to give buyers an incentive to pay you for a longer period of time rather than refinance your loan.

If something came up and the buyers wanted or needed to sell they might just pay off the seller financed loan even if there were pre-payment penalties. However, if you had made the loans assumable, future buyers could take over the loans. By doing this you would have an even better chance of getting payments for the full term of ten years or at least until the pre-payment penalty date had passed. (This is a good argument to have the pre-payment penalty last for the entire length of the loan)

But what if you wanted better odds than that? Or what if you wanted the payments to go on *longer* than the term of the pre-payment penalty or even past the balloon time? How could you structure the note?

Let me now show you the ultimate way to set up your seller financing to accomplish *income for life*.

1. Allow the loan to be *assumed*.
2. Agree to *subordinate* to any other loan on the property.
3. Have the *call date reset* each time someone assumes the loan.

Here is why this loan structure is so important. What it does is let each buyer pass your loan on to any subsequent buyer. The loan is assumed and the ten year clock *resets*!

Let's say you sell a property for $250,000 and let the buyer have a seller financed 2nd lien note of $50,000 and then get a $200,000 1st lien with a lender. You make the loan interest-only so the payment is lower. (There is no mortgage insurance due to the 80% first lien.) You add a 10 year pre-payment penalty of $7,500. (This decreases the chance of refinancing.) You also put a reset clause in your loan and allow the loan to be assumed.

If this buyer wanted to sell after five years, normally your payments would *stop*. But we know you don't want that to happen. Because of how you've now structured the loan another buyer can assume the loan so your payments will continue.

The new buyer's bank doesn't mind because you agree to subordinate to them. (They will be in '1st lien' position on the property) In addition the new buyer now *restarts* the 10 year clock on the loan to you.

This reset should not matter to any new buyers because both they and the previous buyers were only paying interest anyway. The new buyer must either pay the interest, or the full amount is owed to you. In addition, if your loan had not been assumed by the new buyer a new loan for at least the same duration or longer would have been obtained.

Now the *new* buyer has a 10 year pre-payment penalty and *you* get payments for 10 more years. (You have already received five years so now you are up to a possible 15 years of payments.) Next time it sells this happens again and your payment term extends again.

Even if all of these terms are properly set up your seller financed loan might still get paid off. This would occur if any of the buyers ever made loan payments for the full 10 years and then paid off your loan in full when the balloon came. It is rare for someone to stay in a property that long so hopefully it won't happen. If it did, you could go to the buyer and see if they would want to keep making payments and not pay off the balloon. (Or you could even put a renewal option clause in the loan at the beginning)

The other time your loan may get paid off is if the property is sold and the new buyer does not want to assume the loan. At that point you would be paid the $7,500 pre-payment penalty paid and have it to add to your income. (Though it is always a sad day when some of your property-less passive income stops) Hopefully you have seller financed several properties and this is not your only property-less passive income, and/or you will take these funds and invest them in income producing endeavors.

Finally, here are a few more ways to manipulate the loan in your favor. What if you put a fee of one or two percent on the loan if someone assumes it? And, what if you raised the interest rate each time someone assumes it? If these things were included in the loan you would end up with bonus checks every few years plus your loan payments would increase whenever the property re-sold!

In this example you have "Income for Life" plus bonus checks and raises. I can't think of anything much nicer than that. This is why I say the "One Hit Wonder" combined with the "Income for Life" plan has the ability to set you up with passive income for your entire life without property management. This is quite literally "The Highest and Best Real Estate Investment!"

I invite you to join me in the wonderful world of property-less passive income. At the same time you will be helping more people live the

American dream of home ownership. The time for widespread seller financing literacy has come!

Thank you for reading this book. I genuinely care about your success. My highest goal is to create massively successful investors who create win/win deals. Because of this I suggest you read "The Highest and Best Real Estate Investment" book as well as re-read this book so you can become a master of these techniques. Then go out and do some deals!

If you want to learn these concepts one-on-one with me and other investors please join us at one of the numerous seminars I offer on these and many other topics. In addition remember to visit "The Forum" on my website www.mikewatsoninvesting.com and read about what my students and I have been doing in the real estate investing world.

Happy Investing,

Mike Watson

APPENDIX **1**

FREQUENTLY ASKED QUESTIONS

Appendix 1:
Frequently asked Questions

1. How do I get seller financing if there is not any equity in the property?

The loan could be wrapped if it is very close to the value of the property. Or, if the seller is really upside down (more is owed on the property than it is worth) you can do a short sale with the bank by assuming the loan and having the bank lower the amount you would owe. The old owners would still owe the bank the difference but there would not be a foreclosure on their record. Remember to get the "Due on Sale Clause" removed so it can be a "Green" mortgage.

2. If a loan was wrapped and a seller gave me a second wouldn't it be better to compile them into just one mortgage on the property?

The reason for having multiple mortgages on the same property is flexibility. You can read about the benefits of multiple mortgages in the splintering and wrapping sections. The biggest benefit is that you will have options later on down the road that you otherwise would not have. Also, by having multiple loans it keeps the original lender separate from the seller's equity loan. This way you could pay one or the other off at any time without their affecting each other.

3. If I wrap someone's mortgage and the seller is later going to buy another property, will the "wrapped" mortgage count against them for qualifying or will they still be able to qualify for their new loan?

If the mortgage was obtained by an institution that reports to the credit bureaus it *will* count against their credit in applying for a new loan. However, most people forget that the new payments they get from you will count towards their income as well. In essence it is almost a wash. They get the seller financed payment from you as new *income* and the debt from the mortgage still remains. Having that mortgage is not nearly as devastating as you would think in their new loan qualification process.

4. My bank won't give me a first lien if there is a seller financed second lien? How can I create a zero down deal?

This is a question I frequently get in class. The fact is there are many banks that won't do a deal like this. However if you talk with enough banks you *will* find one. The key is to show the bank specifically how you are going to *improve the value* of the property. Another key is to talk with smaller local banks. They are more interested in your community and will have more options as far as allowing these types of deals to go through. It also helps if you can show that the income from the property more than supports the combined payments for the two loans.

5. How do I handle a real estate agent who is involved in a deal and doesn't understand seller financing?

I have run into many real estate agents who are afraid of seller financing. They don't understand it so they are unwilling to "risk" anything by including this when dealing with clients. Usually it is a matter of education. See if you can sit down with those realtors and talk about why it is so good for their sellers. This may be enough to get them to openly work with their sellers using seller financing.

If they go so far as to refuse to show your offer to their sellers (which is not allowed) then make a written offer and request to be present when it is shown to the seller. This is your right as a buyer. Now you can take your time and explain the benefits directly to the seller. Additionally, show the agent how their commission will be paid. (From the buyer's first lien or by the seller directly) Many agents fear seller financing because they believe it will greatly delay or even prevent any commission from being paid.

6. How can you get sellers to do seller financing if they want to do a 1031 exchange with their proceeds?

This is a tricky one. A 1031 tax deferred exchange requires that once a relinquished property is sold, the proceeds must be reinvested into the replacement property no more than 6 months after the first closing. One way you could do seller financing with these transactions would be by closing on the property with a 30 year amortization schedule and a 5.5 month call. This means that you would buy the property, create and enhance the equity; sell it for a profit or refinance it for an equity position before the six months is up.

Next, you would take the proceeds of the refinance or sale, fund the original seller's proceeds and then the original seller would use that money to close on the new replacement property before 180 days expires.

My advice would be to have all of the contracts on all of the properties in place before you name the properties as 1031. This includes your purchase of the original property, the purchase of the seller's next property and even the approval of the new buyer or completely approved refinance loan on the deal. This technique is not for the faint of heart and should be done with professional help and careful consideration.

7. How do you get seller financing from a portion of a partnership if one partner does not want to seller finance?

Suppose three partners equally own (33.3% each) a free and clear $600,000 property. Two want to seller finance and the other does not. You could simply get private money in the amount of $200,000 and then one note for $400,000 or two notes for $200,000. The cash down would pay off the partner who didn't want to seller finance and the other two could then carry a note.

You could even get $300,000 in bank or private financing. With this, $200,000 could go to the partner who wants out and $50,000 each could go to the other two partners. This would give them some cash at closing and leave them each with $150,000 in note receivables.

8. How do I offer properties with seller financing for sale so that I get the most buyers and highest price?

The power of seller financing can be truly harnessed in today's market. The beauty of it is that a seller can offer financing in a market where traditional financing is difficult to obtain. Properties that are offered with financing *in place* for buyers, can and will command a premium.

This is true in any market but is certainly heightened in today's troubled times. Make sure in your advertising that you highlight the fact of easier "qualifying" for the new buyer. Remember you want to qualify your buyers but you also want to have the market be open enough to get a lot of buyers interested.

9. How can the seller get cash at closing and I still get 100% seller financing?

You can have the seller get a second lien on the property from a bank or any other entity or person and then you can wrap both of the loans. That way the seller gets the money from the second lien and you are still getting 100% seller financing. (Or the seller can sell their note right after closing at a small discount)

10. How do you get sellers to agree to a longer call time?

Show them a "4-offer spreadsheet" with an example of a longer call time. This usually does the trick as they see how much money they can make in interest over time. It might also be fun to include a "Truth in Lending" statement that shows a very long term loan. This is the statement a lender is required to show a borrower at closing that shows how much money they are making over the entire time of the loan. Whenever this is shown to me at a closing I feel like crawling under a rock. But the bank is thrilled. Put the seller in the shoes of the bank.

Another way is to convince these sellers that "Wealth with Legs" (payments over a longer period of time), is in their best interest. Receiving payments over a long period of time is a good definition of retirement for many sellers. Additionally, receiving interest and delaying the receipt of principal for many years is a great way to delay capital gains taxes on properties where there is a lot of equity.

11. How do you get a lower interest rate from sellers?

The answer to this is to simply ask, or to just assume they will give it to you. If they are really stuck on a certain rate they may have a critical need to get a certain amount of income. If the deal works, go ahead and give it to them. You can always increase the interest rate even higher and pay them less for the property. Remember you can make the terms fit your side of the deal too.

12. Who should go in the 2nd lien position if I do a wrap, the seller finances some of the equity, and then I get a private capital investor for my down payment? Would it be the seller with his note or my capital investor?

In my opinion it is best to determine who goes in what position by the size of the loan. Therefore if the seller financed note is more than the private capital note then the seller goes in 2nd position. If it is smaller the seller would go in 3rd position behind the private capital note. One thing this does is make all parties compete for the better position by giving you a higher loan amount. When this happens you will be the one to benefit by having to bring *less* to the table!

13. What if I get someone to agree to move their loan to a different property (so I can refinance and raise capital) but I don't own any other properties with equity?

You could give the sellers some terms they can't refuse in order to completely remove the loan from *all* properties. (This is the full de-collateralization, rather than just a re-collateralization or cross-collateralization) Or you could move it to a property that did not have any equity.

Another option is to obtain a collateral partner. I have had partners that put up property as collateral for a loan for a return, instead of investing cash for a return. This works great for someone who has assets and wants to invest but has no cash on hand.

14. How do I get a seller to do a zero interest loan or no payments or both?

I typically have the best luck obtaining these terms when sellers are in a distressed situation. I would hope to come in and save them from disaster in exchange for terms like these. Another way to accomplish this same result without having to negotiate these types of terms is to do an "extended close transaction". In this case you wouldn't close until certain things have been done to the property and during that time you wouldn't have to make payments because you don't yet own the property.

15. When I offer seller financing to a buyer how much down payment should I collect?

The amount of down payment you collect is a very personal decision. My only advice here is that you do not ever do a zero down for a buyer. Even if they are in a great situation right now you never know what may happen and you want them to have some skin in the deal. That way they are motivated to pay you. The cash can be from the buyer's own funds or from a loan they obtain. (As in the "One Hit Wonder")

MWI
INVESTOR TOOLS

Appendix 2:
MWI Investor Tools

Events

MWI Degree Camps...268

MWI Super Camps 270

MWI Mini Camps...270

MWI GUTS Camps 271

Investing Products

Home Study Courses 272

MLS Searches 273

Books 274

Role-Play Series..275

Mike Watson's Inner Circle and Newsletter 276

For more information, and to order any of these MWI Investing Tools:

- **Visit** www.MikeWatsonInvesting.com

- **or call toll-free** 1(866) WATSON-5

MWI DEGREE CAMPS

Degree Camps are taught by Mike Watson.
There are eight MWI Degree Camps on advanced investing topics:

Advanced Seller Financing Degree Camp

Create amazing investing deals with seller financing! Seller financing opens doors for real estate investing and offers huge benefits for the seller. By the end of this camp, Mike Watson will have taught you how to easily negotiate seller financing. This camp will build your confidence, create a vision of options, and revitalize your investments.

Non-Compete Methods, Leverage, and Systems Degree Camp

Learn how to find the deals other investors are missing! You don't have to frantically chase after leads, or compete with other investors. At this camp let Mike Watson teach you how to take control of your investing career through Non-Compete methods. You will learn how to become *the* investing expert in your community, and people will come to you with their investment opportunities.

Creating & Enhancing Equity Degree Camp

Now you can learn Mike Watson's techniques to create instant equity. Mike designed this course to inspire investors to create equity by taking advantage of methods most either never considered or thought impossible.

Cash Flow Degree Camp

The current national real estate market is ripe with cash flow and passive income opportunities! Learn how to turn real estate into an automated and extremely profitable business.

Flips, Fixers, & Flixers Degree Camp

Mike Watson has created a camp to teach his simple techniques to successfully flip, fix or *flix* a property. How would you like to make a large profit on a fixer-upper without doing any work. Hard to believe? It is very possible, and you better enroll for this camp to learn this technique. This is one of Mike's favorite techniques!

Bus Tour Degree Camp

Get out into the field with Mike Watson and personally visit 20+ of Mike's personal investments properties. These deals represent over one million dollars in profits. This is one of the most impactful camps we do for people because you will see these investments up close and personal. There will be no more denying you can invest when you see these deals!

Raising Capital Degree Camp

Raising Capital is vital to investing in today's real estate market. During this powerful camp learn Mike Watson's techniques, and discover how simple raising capital can be. Students leave this camp excited to raise money for their investments, and you will too.

Contracts Degree Camp

Often considered complicated and technical, the subject of contracts is too often neglected. Understanding contracts is fundamental and essential for a successful real estate investor. At this camp, Mike Watson breaks down this subject into an easy to understand format. Learn powerful techniques for preparing and reviewing contracts to get immediate results.

Super Camps

Mike Watson hosts regular Super Camps covering new topics. Some of the recent Super Camps have been:

- The "EVERYTHING CHANGES!" Super Camp
- The "Retire In 5 Years" Super Camp
- The "Any WHERE! Any TIME!" Super Camp
- The "Cash Flow" Super Camp

Super Camps are designed for *new* investors as well as *seasoned MWI students*. They are must-attend events to stay updated on our changing real estate markets. MWI also has Home Study Courses of past Super Camps for sale. Visit our web site to sign up for the next Super Camp!

Mini Camps

The MWI Mini Camps are smaller classes on detailed investing topics. These intimate events are taught by Mike Watson.

Note Buying Mini Camp

At this camp, you will learn how to buy notes from banks and private individuals and sell them for a profit. Become an expert at turning any note receivable into cash.

Property Management Mini Camp

Mike Watson defines Property Management as the "most profitable business in the world". He should know! Mike Watson personally owns hundreds of units, and has an extremely low vacancy rate. Come learn Mike's techniques and make property management one of the most profitable things you do.

GUTS Camps

The MWI GUTS Camps are limited to a small number of students to ensure the greatest level of personal attention is given to each student who attends. These events are taught by Mike's Pro Coaches.

The Portfolio Tour GUTS Camp

Be one of the few students fortunate enough to visit the office of J&K Interests and receive two days of training from two of Mike's most successful students, Jim Stephens and Kevin Liu. Visit the partnership properties that Jim and Kevin are partnering with MWI on.

Deal Evaluation GUTS Camp

Imagine the value of spending two days with Josh Escobedo of the Deal Maker's Division to discuss each aspect of evaluating and processing a real estate deal! Attend this event and you will receive answers to your deal evaluation questions in an intimate setting. You will complete more transactions in less time by eliminating guesswork when evaluating a deal.

Property Management GUTS Camp

This personalized camp is taught by Mike's own property management team. Learn about contracts, tenants, property maintenance and more. You will also learn how to train others to help with your property management. At this event, you will also receive a complete set of forms and tools needed to be a successful property manager.

HOME STUDY COURSES

"Cash Flow" Home Study Course

Learn why our current market is ripe with cash flow opportunities! Learn how to start creating passive income right away. Contains 12 audio discs and all course materials.

Any WHERE! Any TIME!" Home Study Course

Join Mike Watson and learn how to find and evaluate profitable investing deals in ANY market at ANY time! Includes: 15 Audio CD's, with over 18 hours of instruction with Mike, and all camp materials.

"Retire In 5 Years" Home Study Course

Learn how to retire in 5 years or less! With this Home Study Course, you can learn the system that is creating an early retirement for investors around the country! Your Home Study Course includes: 16 audio discs, with over 22 hours of life-changing instruction from Mike Watson, with all notes included.

"EVERYTHING CHANGES"
Home Study Course - DVD Set

Take advantage of the same strategies that have inspired many real estate investors to create lasting change and wealth through real estate investing. Your set includes: 4 DVD's, over 20 hours of instruction with Mike Watson, and presentations from Mike's most successful students.

The "Becoming Your Own Best Client" Home Study Course

A live recording of one of Mike Watson's powerful introductory camps. Mike teaches you how to achieve freedom and become your own best client. A great way to internalize all of Mike's proven strategies at your own pace! Learn with Mike in your car, office, or at home! Includes 18 audio CD's, and over 24 hours of instruction.

MLS Searches

Top Multi-Family MLS Searches

These are Mike Watson's most productive multi-family MLS searches. Search the MLS with Mike Watson, and watch how he evaluates deals. Learn Mike's secrets to find properties everyone else is missing! Just insert the CD-ROM into your computer, and watch and listen to Mike as he searches the MLS.

Top Single-Family MLS Searches

These are Mike Watson's most productive single-family MLS searches. Search the MLS with Mike Watson, and watch how he evaluates deals. Learn Mike's secrets to find great deals everyone else is missing! Just insert the CD-ROM into your computer, and watch and listen to Mike as he searches the MLS.

Books

The "Highest and Best" Real Estate Investment!

The first comprehensive book on Mike Watson's entire investing system. Written by Mike Watson and Jennifer Hawkins, this book dives into the Foundation to Success. Learn the skills and systems you need for successful investing in any market condition! 348 pages.

Liberation - Will You Survive or Thrive?

40 Inspirational quotes and dialog by Mike Watson, with Jennifer Hawkins. Do you notice you are either not taking action or not getting the results you want?

Do you find it hard to stay passionate about your life on a day to day basis? Mike Watson is a master when it comes to being passionate and taking action. He truly lives his motto "Err on the side of action". With this book, you can own and access a little part of Mike's strength and motivation every day. Full color, 95 pages.

The Do-It-Yourself Guide to Property Maintenance for Those That *Don't* Do-It-Themselves

Mike Watson presents a step-by-step Property Maintenance book by Nicholas Escobedo and St. John Holloway. Book includes instruction on everything from managing a property to dealing with emergencies.

60 Days to Success Planner

A powerful daily investment planner developed by Mike Watson. Includes 60 days of daily investment tasks designed to turn you into a successful investor. The perfect way to get started, and stay on track to accomplish your investing goals.

Role-Play Series

Power Team Role-Play Audio CDs

This role-play is a *must-have* for anyone who wants to start a Power Team! Contains 2 Audio CDs. Join Mike Watson at a role-play of an "introductory" Power Team meeting or "Open House". Mike shares his Power Team vision with a room full of real estate professionals. He breaks down Power Teams, and gives the attendees overwhelming reasons to become members of the brand-new team. With this role-play, you will understand how to conduct your own successful first Power Team meeting or Open House.

Capital Raising Role-Play Audio CD

Join Mike Watson on a detailed role-play of a recent Capital Raising phone call. Mike breaks down the investing process with a potential investor, and gives them overwhelming reasons to invest their hard-earned money in his deals. He resolves multiple concerns from the investor, and gets them excited to invest in his deal.

Overcoming Seller Financing Objections Role-Play Audio CDs

Join Mike Watson as he shows you how to overcome common Seller Financing objections. In this role play Mike works with six sellers and gives them overwhelming reasons to seller finance their properties. This role-play is a *must-have* for anyone who wants to master Seller Financing! Contains 2 audio CDs.

Mike Watson's
Inner Circle and Newsletter

Inner Circle

 Mike Watson's Inner Circle is an exclusive group of investors who receive monthly training and updates from Mike Watson. Members receive a monthly subscription to the "INVEST NOW" newsletter, as well as cutting-edge investing techniques directly from Mike and the MWI coaches.

Inner Circle members enjoy exclusive Webinar training as well as access to a massive online library of investing training, media, tools, and other MWI resources.

"INVEST NOW" Newsletter

 The "INVEST NOW" Newsletter is the official publication of Mike Watson's Inner Circle. This monthly newsletter is mailed to subscribers, and includes an investing message from Mike Watson, and other reports and articles from MWI coaches and investors. The "INVEST NOW" newsletter is the perfect way to stay in touch with the constantly changing real estate market.